STRAIGHT MAN

1970s Interviews & Photos From Vancouver's Underground Press
The Georgia Straight • The Grape • The Terminal City Express

By Rick McGrath

The Terminal Press
2014

This one is for Catherine...

Johnny Winter and Mississippi Fred McDowell jamming at Vancouver's Purple Steer Club, 1971.   Rick McGrath photo

The Terminal Press
135 MacPherson Avenue
Toronto, Ontario
M5R 1W9
Canada

Copyright © 2014 The Terminal Press.
All rights reserved.

Editorial Consultant: Karl Siegler
Design: Rick McGrath

Set in 10pt Minion Pro

ISBN: 978-0-9918665-2-6

No part of this book may be reproduced by any means, in any media, electronic or mechanical, including motion picture film, video, photocopy, recording, or any other information storage retrieval system, without prior permission in writing from the publisher.

Stuart H. Clugston photos Copyright © Stuart H. Clugston 2014.
All rights reserved.

Acknowledgements
The publisher gratefully thanks Rob Frith of Vancouver's astounding Neptoon Records for Stuart Clugston's photos of the 1971 Led Zeppelin Vancouver press conference, and for art from the Rob Frith collection of posters and memorabilia.
Visit Rob at neptoon.com

The Interview Setlist:

Chicago Transit Authority 7
Pentangle 10
Mitch Ryder & Detroit 13
Kim Simmonds 17
Gordon Lightfoot 19
Van Morrison 22
Fleetwood Mac 27
Crowbar 30
Elton John 32
35 Crowbar
41 Led Zeppelin
47 Captain Beefheart
52 Red Robinson
58 High Flying Bird
60 Luke Gibson
63 John Lyle
65 Al Neil
70 Captain Beefheart

Bonus Tracks:

Bob Dylan & The Band Pix 73
ShaNaNa Pix 75
Van Morrison Pix 77
Larry Coryell Pix 81
Joan Baez Pix 82
Tim Buckley Pix 83
The Tubes Pix 86
John Fahey Pix 89
Tom Rapp Album Review 92
Rolling Stones *Gimme Shelter* Movie Review 95
Rolling Stones *Cocksucker Blues* Movie Review 98
The Prisoner DVD Box Set Review 101
Sam Fuller *Shock Corridor* Movie Review 111
The Velvet Underground Pix 115
The Who Autographs 116

Underground Days...

It was in the fall of 1969 when I wandered down to the then-gritty Gastown area of Vancouver, found a decrepit hole of a storefront in the side of an old brick facade, made out a faded sign that barely said *Georgia Straight* through the dusty window, smiled as I noted the *Sorry, We're Open* sign, gingerly pushed open the creaking door and found myself in a long gap of a corridor twixt the window sill and an equally long barricade of a store counter. The air smelled like patchouli and cockroaches in a bowl of dank.

"Yeah?" A young face appeared above the shabby wooden counter. "Ya want some *Straights*? We're out." She was referring to how the paper supported itself outside of corner store sales and the odd paid advertisement. The deal was basic capitalism: anybody could wander in and buy copies of *The Georgia Straight*—Vancouver's then underground newspaper—at the wholesale rate of 15 cents each, and then sell them on the street for the printed 25 cent retail price. In 1969 ten cents could buy you—well, one-fiftieth of a nickel bag. Or a small beer. You do the math. I indicated no, no papers. None of that hippy work. I was interested in a job. Music critic. Rock reviewer. She flashed me the sign of one raised eyebrow and disappeared through one of those chittering glass bead curtains to return a discernible time later.

"Follow me." She flipped up the horizontal door that made a canyon in The Wall of a counter and I sidled the gap to the Inner Sanctum. Through the annoying beads we went and then down a center hallway flanked by cubicles cobbled together with rough two by fours and cheap plywood—a sort of Japanese restaurant as imagined by Max Ernst—to an unoffice where my hostess waved me in to meet with Al Sorensen, *The Straight's* entertainment editor.

As luck would have it, Al had recently convinced *Georgia Straight* publisher/editor Dan McLeod to bankroll a special monthly tabloid called *Rip-Off*, an insert devoted to sex, drugs & rock 'n' roll. Yes, there was a message there. But this tabloid had a lot of pages to fill and there was not a lot of copy to fill it. Sorensen needed content for readers. I needed empty space to write my way into the music scene. The universe unfolded.

Al gave me a copy of The Doors' *Morrison Hotel* to review and away we went. I did various freelance interviews and reviews until the summer of 1970 when Al left and the entertainment editor gig came to me. *Rip-Off* had succumbed to a lack of ad revenues, and my revolutionary rôle was now reduced to filling a couple pages of each issue with, well, whatever radical youth culture taste-defining stuff I wanted. Or could find, which led me to freelancers such as classical rocker Mike Quigley, film critic Kirk Tougas, and jazz writer Robert Rouda. In the end Mike Quigley hung around the longest, joining me for interviews and contributing his *Mikey Music* column, with the odd reprint or freelancer chipping in. I did what I liked: rock concert and record reviews, with interviews whenever I could.

This rock *gadda-da-vida* went on peacefully until the spring of 1972, when all hell broke loose over ownership of *The Straight*, and most of the staff self-righteoused off to kick communal ass with an alternate underground paper. I was one of them. We published a paper called *The Georgia Grape*, which soon changed to *The Grape*, and then soon after that most of the grapers became gripers and left to start up another alternate alternate underground newspaper, *The Terminal City Express*.

By this time *The Straight's* original talent pool had disintegrated into various warring camps and I had already started to drift away from the whole underground press scene. OK, fade away. My last interview was with Captain Beefheart in March of 1973. And that was that.

When I look back now, the high point of those years has to be interviewing Led Zeppelin: it's tough to beat a night where you watch the concert—*onstage*—from behind Page's frontstage speaker banks—*he was 20 feet away*—before talking to Robert Plant at the moment he turned 23 and hearing the one-and-only telling of how the group survived the Milan concert fire and subsequent police riot. That kind of a night tends to stick with you. My other favourite conversations were with the mysterious Van Morrison, who had a reputation for never giving interviews at all, the wonderfully wacky Don Van Vliet, Hall of Fame DJ Red Robinson, and the highly energetic jazzman, Al Neil.

One thing more. I'm also a footnote for simply leaving *The Straight* when I did: the scruffy Irishman who replaced me as rock reviewer in 1972 turned out to be none other than Sir Bob Geldof. Yes, I take full credit for enabling his success.

Rick McGrath
Toronto, 2014

Chicago: Peaceful Revolution

The Gardens Auditorium, Vancouver, April 1970

BEFORE THE DEATH by misadventure of Terry Kath, Chicago's brilliant guitarist, this was an amazing group to see live. They had it all: upbeat stage presence, guitar hero, good voices, killer drummer, and a kick-ass repertoire of songs, the best of which allowed the group to do stretch-out fusion jazzrock, horns blaring until Kath lasered in with his incendiary playing and brought it all back home.

This, my first *Georgia Straight* interview, was done in a dressing room with my fellow scribbler Mike Quigley amid the confusion of Illinois Speed Press preparing to go onstage (both bands shared the rather cramped dressing room), groupies, and only about fifteen minutes worth of time to talk with James Pankow, Chicago's trombonist.

Rick McGrath: The liner notes on your latest album, Chicago II, talk about the revolution. What revolution is that?

James Pankow: It's a peaceful revolution. I mean, we're not in the position to tell people what to do, but this country is obviously in a state of turmoil because the younger generation is not happy with the way the older generation's running the country. Violence is not the answer, although people have had to go to extreme means to get their points across because they aren't being listened to. What the answer is, I can't say.

We're aware of the situation like a lot of people are, and we let people know it through our music. In that way our album is dedicated to the revolution in the fact that we're aware of the political upheaval in this country and if we can make people more aware of it, like we are, then maybe better understanding can come out of the whole thing—better communication.

McGrath: Last year the group's image was rather anti-political. Any reason for the change?

James Pankow: Well, the reason I said that we were anti-political is that we didn't like to think of ourselves as a political group. We thought of ourselves as a musical group because the music is what we're in the business for—it's our life. But last year things weren't coming to a head like they are now. Kids weren't as involved as they are now because they didn't have to be. Kennedy was assassinated. Martin Luther King was assassinated. The hopes for the younger generation were gotten rid of. And about the time of those assassinations, when the outright revolution began, things were not as stormy as they are now.

We just wanted people to know that we're aware of what's going on over the country, all over the world, and we say it in the music. We don't want to tell kids to go burn down universities and break windows and things like this, because that's not the answer to anything. It's just a matter of communication—people have to talk to one another rather than criticize. It brings us down when we go from town to town and see uptightness and bad things going on around the country, and it affects us, our emotions and our thoughts. The best release for these thoughts and emotions is in the music, so we say it in the music. And in that way our music is dedicated to the revolution in the way that people may become more aware of what's going on in this country and they may begin to communicate more.

Mike Quigley: You also had an idea of a musical community. Can you explain that a bit more?

James Pankow: We're like a family—like brothers. The same personnel have been together for about three and a half years now, and we stick together socially and musically. As far as the "musical community" to refer to is concerned, well, it's set up like a business and within this corporation there's a production company, a management company, a publishing company, and other little things, and some day we hope to be in the position to give other musicians a break like we got.

McGrath: Like Frank Zappa's Bizarre organization...?

James Pankow: Yeah. In the future we'd like to build a studio, possibly in the Northwestern U.S.—somewhere in the mountains, and record other groups that we have an interest in, and give them the chance that we had, because there's a need for a cultural revolution as well as a political revolution. I mean people are listening to better music in general. Rock and roll is no longer 1-4-5; it's no longer simple music. It's becoming a legitimate music form and it deserves advancement just as any

music form. If we can help other groups out someday, fine. We aren't in a position to do it now.

Quigley: Do you envision it as a North American version of Apple?

James Pankow: I suppose you couald, to make the analogy.

Quigley: Chicago II has a lot of classical music on it. Do you think you'll carry on in that trend?

James Pankow: Not necessarily. It just happened that we were in that direction about the time of the recording of that album. It's hard to say what direction the music is going in—whatever comes out at any particular time, that's what comes out. We may go into a country & western vein—any particular music we happen to be in at that time. We try to be as versatile as possible without getting cluttered, so to speak. We don't want to be ultra-commercial, we don't want to prostitute ourselves, but on the other hand we don't want to become so complex that we burn ourselves out of the industry. Like The Mothers. The Mothers had a very musical thing going but their approach was a little too heavy, a little too quick for the mass media to accept, and they kind of burned themselves out. Zappa got so frustrated that he closed the band down.

Quigley: On Chicago II you have four classical-like cuts that are orchestrated. They're the one thing I really couldn't get into. What are you trying to do with those cuts?

James Pankow: Don't you think they're musical?

Quigley: Yeah, but the only interesting part is where you're interpolating little outbursts like Stravinsky.

James Pankow: The first five minutes of that tune is an instrumental, an orchestration by Peter Matz. The tune is a love ballad written by Terry, our guitar player. The orchestration, which is a prelude for the tune, just kind of sets you up for the tune. We like it because it contributes to the overall effect of the album. It's a little different, a little more musical than the first album. We don't like to get into misrepresentation—we don't like to make people think we have violins with us and all that sort of thing; to do a big orchestrated Garry Puckett sort of thing (to drop a name). We just thought that one tune deserved a little extra, a little orchestration, because it meant a lot to the guitar player and he wanted it to be orchestrated.

McGrath: You seem to be on the road a lot. Do you get to spend much time in the studio?

James Pankow: Well, yes, lately we've been devoting most of our time to live performances, just playing as much as we can and playing for as many people as we can. We've been recording in between the road shots, and yes, we've been very busy.

McGrath: Do you have any network TV spots coming up?

James Pankow: We've refused to do American television because of bad audio. If we did American television, we'd do it live—we don't go in for the lip-synching, and up to now American sound engineers have not been able to capture any sound experience well, including Blood, Sweat and Tears, who I saw on the *Ed Sullivan Show*. They sounded bad because the engineers didn't know what they were doing. We did a lot of TV shows in Europe when we were over there because the European engineers are into live recording, live video tape, and it came off very well.

McGrath: Yeah. Santana was on Ed Sullivan and the engineers just didn't have a clue as to what was happening.

James Pankow: Right. We did NBC's *First Tuesday* and it'll be on in April or May. We did that because it's a documentary, and that's a story of the group, who we are, what we are, how we live at home, how we live on the road.

They followed us around on the road, getting out of bed in the morning, rehearsing, shooting the bull, brushing our teeth, going to the store—it shows us as we are from day to day. It's not a phony thing—it's us, and because it's a documentary, because of the presentation, we did that show. But we won't do any variety shows.

McGrath: Looking ahead a bit, do you anticipate doing any more rock festivals this summer in light of Altamont?

James Pankow: Well, you can't judge them all by one or a couple. The *Atlantic City Pop Festival* and the *Atlanta Pop Festival* were both excellent. They were very well organized, and the sound systems were more than adequate.

All the people there—up to 50,000—got to hear everything that was presented because of the setup. So you can't judge them all by a couple of bad ones. I personally have nothing against rock festivals. I think it's a good way of reaching a large number

of people. We were going to do the *Toronto Revival* with John Lennon in April, but that was cancelled.

Quigley: Are you working on a third album now?

James Pankow: We're recording in June so we can have a third album out by Christmas of this year. It's going to be kind of tight since we'll be on the road all through May and it's hard to write material on the road—you have to write it at home in most cases.

So we're going to be kind of busy, getting our material ready for the third album as well as getting ourselves together to play on the road.

McGrath: Have you thought of taping any of your live performances for an album?

James Pankow: Well, the mobile units that record you on the road are effective if you've got a small group, a four or a three piece group. But when you have this many pieces, everything has to be miked in such a way that everything becomes an involved, difficult process to pick up the seven pieces with the brass in such a way that it'll be recordable.

So we're restricting ourselves to the studio for now. Maybe someday we'll think of a live performance.

Pentangle: Round the Roses

Queen Elizabeth Theatre, Vancouver, May, 1970

PENTANGLE? SURE. I knew Bert Jansch from my folkie days, and I knew he had more than a passing influence on Donovan. Given their dedication to acoustic music, I thought they'd be serious as hell, but they turned out to be hard-drinking, polite, funny, erudite and eager to jump all over Jimmy Page. Jansch, the most dissipated, was funniest, cracking jokes and only getting serious—passionate—at the end when I tried to get them to talk about their music. The group had just completed a fun-filled six-week North American tour and Vancouver was the band's last gig. A time to let loose. After the show I made it backstage and managed to ferret out John Renbourn, Bert Jansch and Jacqui McShee. After a few mandatory beers, the tape started rolling...

Rick McGrath: I heard you had some fun at the border.

Bert Jansch: We came through very smashed, we were all really drunk—it was half past two in the morning. We went to the customs counter and a geezer was going (grimaces) and we were going (smiles insanely)—it was so ridiculous.

Jacqui McShee: He was demanding money.

McGrath: Money?

Bert Jansch: Yeah, we had to put down a deposit on all our gear.

Jacqui McShee: In case we sell them here, you have to give them money. So you have to pay them a hundred dollars and they say because it's after office hours you have to pay them another ten, please. Which we won't get back, but we'll get the hundred back in about six months, if you're good.

McGrath: That sounds odd.

Bert Jansch: Actually, I thought it was very unusual, because, one, the guy who was doing the actual, supposedly, looking in your cases was, actually, drunk.

Jacqui McShee: Because he kept looking, but he couldn't and anything and he kept writing things up and crossing them out and writing them again, and his spelling was so damn bad...

Bert Jansch: And that old bird, remember?

Jacqui McShee: She was young, about eighteen, and she had that coat down to there...

Bert Jansch: ...no, not her, another bird, she had nothing to do with customs, she was just there. An old, old bird. She had nothing, you know, nothing, and there she was, on the board, just sitting on the bench...

Jacqui McShee: I didn't see her, are you sure?

Bert Jansch: That's Customs for you: an old slag sitting there trying to chat with you going through (laughs). Anyway, (looks at me) what were you talking about?

McGrath: Pentangle. You've been around for three years...

John Renbourn: Yes.

McGrath: And the interesting thing about the group is its sophisticated musical sense. How do you get it together?

John Renbourn: That depends what we're going to do. The traditional songs that we do are generally ones that Jacqui or Bert know, or that Bert and myself and Jacqui know. The other songs are generally ones that Bert writes.

McGrath: How do the songs come together?

John Renbourn: When we arrange songs, it's generally worked out in parts. I generally work out harmony parts.

McGrath: What about things other than Pentangle. Terry Cox does a lot of session work, what about you?

John Renbourn: Terry does any sessions that come along. He's a studio musician most of the time.

Bert Jansch: Rock and Roll player.

John Renbourn: I used to do some, but I really get brought down with them.

McGrath: And that leaves you with?

John Renbourn: Things to do on my own. Like early music, early folk music. That's a gas, for me. Like I dig Sandy Bull, from Boston.

McGrath: Bert, you said Rock and Roll player. Do you play any?

Bert Jansch: Not me. I'm your complete folk type. I'm your actual folk (laughs). All the others (waves hand) are ultra genius guitar jazz players, they're the incredible rhythm jazz section. I'm just your simple Donovan at heart...

Jacqui McShee: Noooo....

McGrath: Did you ever play with Donovan?

John Renbourn: Bert never played with Donovan. Donovan used to play exactly like Bert, he learned a lot of Bert's things. That's why it sounds like Bert playing. He recorded a lot of Bert's songs.

Bert Jansch: What he used to do is send his managers around while I was drunk out me mind in a pub and say, "Look, sign this bit of paper", and I'd go (groans) and sign.

McGrath: So you never played on his albums?

Bert Jansch: No, it wasn't me. Look, you listen to Led Zeppelin. They do it on *Black Water Side*.

McGrath: They called it Black Mountain Side.

Bert Jansch: (laughs). That's my song.

Jacqui McShee: Pinch.

McGrath: Yeah, I see. Jimmy Page even plays it the same way: he sits down and he gets an old battered guitar and he gets all hunched over...

Bert Jansch: I don't do that, do I? Get an old battered guitar and play...

Jacqui McShee: No, he means he's got a special guitar for the song. Actually I think it's a very rude thing to do. Pinch somebody else's thing and credit it to yourself. It annoys me.

McGrath: You'd think Page wouldn't have to do that.

Jacqui McShee: In all the English papers at home he's always talking about Bert. Says he's influenced. I mean, why say that and then put something on an LP and say Jimmy Page?

McGrath: I recognize many of the traditional effects you incorporate. The English folk ballad seems quite further advanced than the typical North American folk song.

John Renbourn: Some of the old ballads are amazingly complicated. But there's a lot of the traditional ballads around and they're being revived, like a Pete Seeger type thing here. But you can hear people like Doc Watson.

McGrath: So the songs are easy to find?

Bert Jansch: No, we create them (laughs).

McGrath: Your jazz sound—does it just happen?

Bert Jansch: I don't think we do anything consciously, do we?

Jacqui McShee: No. I don't think so either. I mean, that's the way we got together, wasn't it?

Bert Jansch: Consciously?

Jacqui McShee: No, I mean I'm saying, unconsciously, it's always been like that. That's the way Danny plays, that's the way Terry plays.

Bert Jansch: They're very jazz influenced.

McGrath: Does that account for the jazz-folk thing you get going?

John Renbourn: Well, what happens, if we use a traditional tune, what Danny and Terry put down is essentially a jazz slanted thing, particularly with Terry using a drum kit instead of a hand drum.

McGrath: What about the sitar number?

John Renbourn: We only use it on one song from our last album.

McGrath: You opened tonight with an old Jaynettes number "Sally Go Round The Roses", a cut from Basket of Light. How did that song happen, it's fairly obscure.

John Renbourn: That song was hardly worked out at all, we did it more or less in the studio. It's only a blues thing, but it's nice.

McGrath: What's going to happen after the tour, in England?

John Renbourn: Well, we've got to take a rest. There's festivals and things. We've been trying to cancel out a lot of things, you know, just not do it. There's a lot of things happening, like the concert at the Isle of Wight. We'll be there. There's a festival here at the moment, isn't there?

McGrath: Yes, one called Strawberry Mountain, except it's an island.

John Renbourn: Someone said Albert King was there...

McGrath: No, Albert Collins. He was here last fall with Bo Diddley and Little Richard.

John Renbourn: Oh wow. That's amazing. A lot of places we've played have just had blues festivals. We come in and they've just had every guy that's available. We've always just missed them. I'd love to get round to one. See Robert Williams or Sun House.

McGrath: What about the current music scene in England?

John Renbourn: Well, it's pretty good. Fairport Convention were over here. But there are a lot of good groups. And it's changed a lot; a lot of people that I used to know that would be folk singers have now got groups together and are doing wild things.

Bert Jansch: Is this an underground station you're doing this for?

McGrath: No, it's an underground newspaper.

Bert Jansch: I thought it was underground radio.

McGrath: No, we haven't got there yet.

Bert Jansch: Your newspaper got a name?

McGrath: It's called the Georgia Straight.

Bert Jansch: Georgia Straight?

McGrath: It's a pun.

Bert Jansch: I don't get it (laughs).

McGrath: It's a local play on words... the channel of water beside Vancouver is called Georgia Strait... s-t-r-a-i-t... we spell our Georgia Straight... s-t-r-a-i-g-h-t in the cool sense....

Bert Jansch: I still don't get it (laughs).

McGrath: OK, guys. What about people who have never heard Pentangle? How would you turn them on?

Jacqui McShee: The best way, I think is just to listen to the music. Actually we don't talk much about ourselves.

McGrath: Well, that's a definition of the group's musical ability.

Jacqui McShee: Yes, well, the thing is when you've been together as a band for over three years and when you're together like that—when you think about most of the groups that are going, they might last a year and then they break up and another group breaks up and then they combine and you get sort of satellite groups around one group. When you've been playing together you get to know each other not only as a person but musically as well. Just knowing.

McGrath: I'm trying to get you to come up with a self definition.

Bert Jansch: It's impossible. No one has ever done it yet. There's one thing we never talk about, music. We don't. We never talk music to each other. You understand? It's like, we talk about what we're going to do next. Where we're going, what bars we're going to visit, whether we can have a game of golf at all, or who won the football game. We never talk about music, never. You talk about everything else, but never music.

The only time we ever talk about music is to say "Let's have a rehearsal" and that's it, we get together and play. If anything comes out there you go. Other than that you don't talk, you know? Cause you don't need to.

And we find it hard to talk to anyone else about music cause we just don't.

Mitch Ryder: Just Out There Somewhere

Holiday Inn, Vancouver, July, 1970

MY ONE AND ONLY co-interview with *Georgia Straight* Entertainment Editor Al Sorensen, done a month before he left the paper. Mitch Ryder and his new group played The Commodore Ballroom and then hung around Vancouver for a few days while we set Mitch up for a benefit concert. This tape was made one afternoon in a smoky room...

Rick McGrath: I heard you guys almost got kicked outta here... five cops showed up.

Mitch Ryder: Oh, it was just ridiculous. Worse than you can imagine, man. Here's some people going down the hall with their little kid and shit, just checking in early in the morning, looking forward to some sleep, and some fucking long-haired, red-headed motherfucker was walking down the hall with his prick hanging out... walks by and says "Hi" like nothing was going on, right?

And 10 minutes later some chick's running down the end of the hall—she's being raped by two guys—and they forcibly drag her back in. There's all kinds of screams and noise, pot odours flooding the hall, you know, musical instruments playing, naked chicks out there (points to the balcony), one of the guys shit, put it in a bag and threw it out into the street. The Bible's been tossed out already—every sacrilegious move that could be made has been made. And the topper was last night. We were hungry, man, so Harry went down and made me a sandwich, and he picked himself a breakfast in the kitchen after it was closed. Went down the back way and cased it out—figured out how—you almost didn't get caught, didja?

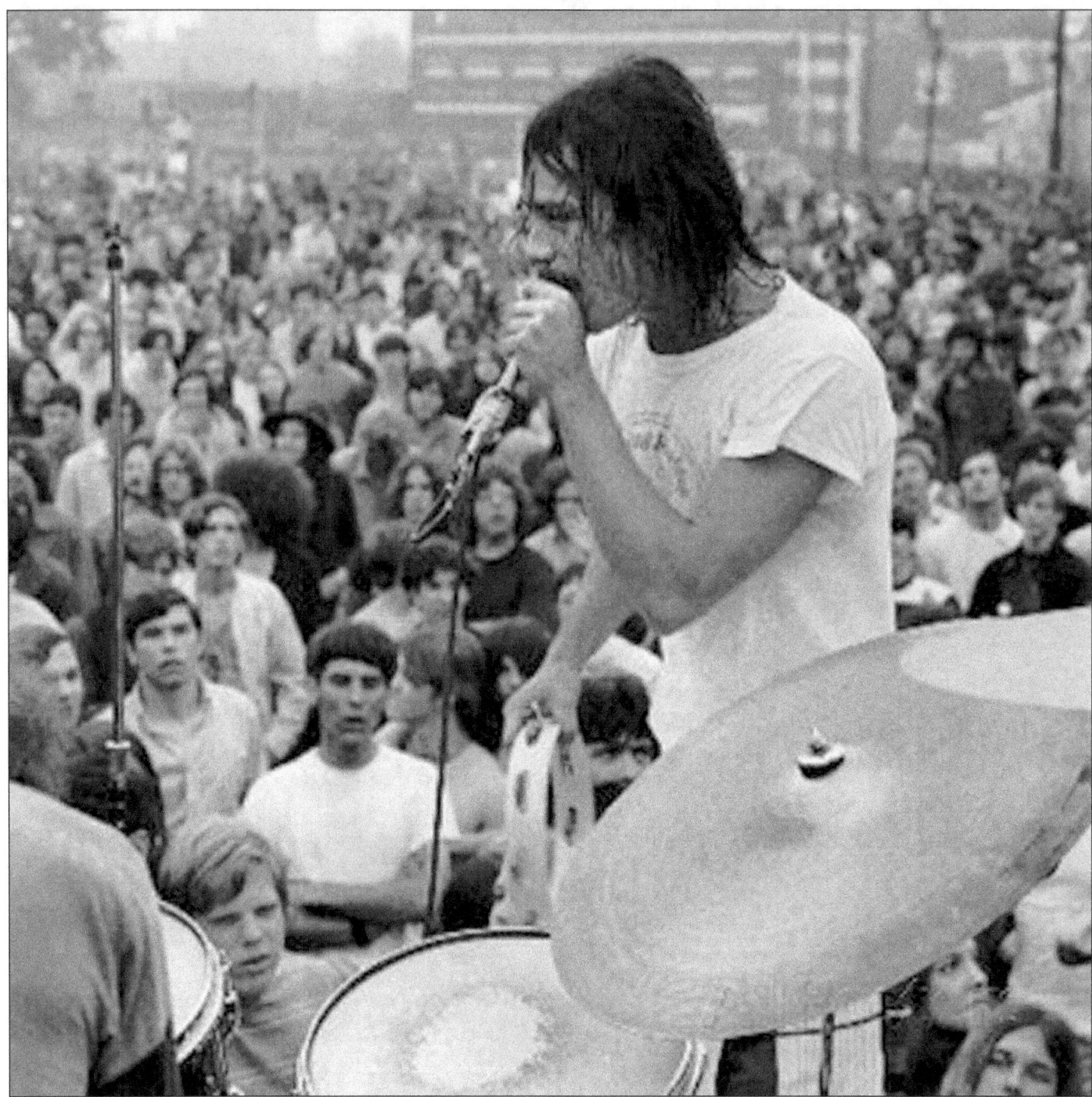

Harry Phillips (keyboards): Yeah, but when I was trucking I was getting a blueberry pie outta the—you know, where the counters and shit are, and the, you know, the dude that walks around with the clock and shit?

McGrath: The watchman...

Harry Phillips: Yeah, he come truckin up there, man, and we seen him and we split. It was pretty crazy. He got all uptight over four chicken salad sandwiches to be exact, and a couple of eggs, piece of toast...

Mitch Ryder: I don't think it was a matter of not being able to pay. There was just no food. He didn't understand.

Al Sorensen: It said in the paper today that only 300 people have seen you in the last three days...

Mitch Ryder: Yeah, but last night was a pretty choice crowd, so that kind of made up for it. Transient assholes. "Hi, man, what do you do? Oh, I'm with the, ahh... Melancholy Float Fuck, you know, we're from Cuba"... or something. You know these people in off the boat. I got some honey, though, man.

Sorensen: It also said that your manager expects to lose something like $10,000...

Mitch Ryder: It's possible, yeah. That would be the best in a long time.

Sorensen: What's he losing it on? The Commodore Ballroom or the band?

Mitch Ryder: Both.

McGrath: It wasn't advertised worth a shit.

Mitch Ryder: All I can see is the potential of that fucking place, as far as it becoming a ballroom, you know? Do you have to be only 19 to drink there?

McGrath: Yeah.

Mitch Ryder: Wow. That place would go nuts, man.

Sorensen: You're going to be recording an album soon.

Mitch Ryder: In Chicago, at RCA.

Sorensen: What sort of material are you going to be doing?

Mitch Ryder: A lot of it's original. We've been working on the album here—but we've worked up three tunes so far and they're all original. And then there's the fourth one, that Lou Reed song, *Rock N' Roll*.

Sorensen: He said he's written a new one called Nobody Loves You When You're Old & Gay.

Mitch Ryder: Old and gay—just wondering how long it would take for that song to get out of the mind. I'm sure it's contemplated many times.

Sorensen: Did you ever meet him?

Mitch Ryder: Yeah, and he was very thrilled about me doing the song.

Sorensen: I've read he's living at home with his parents.

Mitch Ryder: I don't know about that, but I know he's not working with the Velvet Underground and they're doing a tour.

Sorensen: Tell us about your recording of CC Rider and Little Latin Lupe Lu.

Mitch Ryder: Well, cutting them was 1965, but the first hit was like in 1966, 1967 and early 1968. But after that we broke the chain and were no more.

McGrath: Did you put out any other records?

Mitch Ryder: All kinds of records, all the time. My own producer just managed this "write-together-some-more-bullshit-junk" out of this big catalogue and put out another album. That's like "the greatest of what we almost threw away, but kept just in case we needed it."

Sorensen: Little Latin Lupe Lu was live, wasn't it?

Mitch Ryder: Well, *Jenny, Take a Ride* was live, as live as it could be. Sang and played at the same time, recorded it in stereo and mixed it on a two-track. *Little Latin Lupe Lu* was—well, there were people there—they were live because of the energy that went into them at the time. Whoever was in the studio was always included and like that. They had a unique sound, yeah, and I think the band is responsible for that.

Sorensen: Is your new band in the same space?

Mitch Ryder: No, they're not. But they carry the same spirit.

Sorensen: Who wrote them?

Mitch Ryder: Mostly John Badanjek (the drummer) and me.

Sorensen: What about the album you recorded for Stax?

Mitch Ryder: It was interesting. I'll always like it and I'll always appreciate having done it. And I'll always wish it could be done again under better circumstances some day. I don't get to pick my producer—they assign one to me. That's the only one I found acceptable.

They had all kinds of weird people—they wanted Jeff Berry to do me, and Steed, you know? I was down there basically because I had faith in Booker T., not because I was there to make an album or because I was supposed to make an album, and I should have treated it like that.

Sorensen: How did the album do?

Mitch Ryder: It didn't do well for a number of reasons. I thought it wasn't mixed properly, and I thought Steve Cropper and myself didn't take the time for the album that we should have taken. Every time I listen to it I'd find out what was wrong with it in my mind.

You see, we sat down with all their writers and that's the way we would do the songs. They were written at the moment, most of them. The whole thing was just incredible and I got to see The Stax, you know, Machine. We visualized the album as being like—I wanted it to come off more like an Otis Redding kind of thing, you know, with those tunes, and they wanted it to come off. God knows how, because they had respect for me as a musician, as an artist, so they were willing to work with me. It's just—the album itself is just out there somewhere. I don't think you can really tell what went wrong with it—can't describe it. I've tried and it doesn't mean anything. I'll always treasure it, OK?

McGrath: OK. So, how are things in Detroit?

Mitch Ryder: Pretty funky, probably. We sure wish we were back there. This is the longest we've been out in a long time, or will be.

Sorensen: How long is that?

Mitch Ryder: Another month.
Sorensen: Your manager has to put up with your wives.

Mitch Ryder: With our wives? Oh yeah. I guess in his mind it's not even putting up. It's just, you know, allowing it to happen and try not to get too involved.

W.R. Cooke (bass & vocals): Fuck! I wish he would tell me where mine was.

Mitch Ryder: I think there's a message for you to call her at my place.

W.R. Cooke: Oh yeah?

Mitch Ryder: Yeah.

Steve Hunter (lead guitar): Hey, you got a smoke, Billy?

Mitch Ryder: Yeah. I don't have any American cigarettes. Are you burning hash on my American cigarettes?

McGrath: You can buy Kool filters in Vancouver.

(Toke, toke)

Harry Phillips: Get in there! (cough, cough)

Mitch Ryder: Maybe we should get Bee's pipe, man.

W.R. Cooke: Oh, fuck... I dropped that piece.

McGrath: Is this a switchblade?

W.R. Cooke: No.

McGrath: Chopsticks? Portable chopsticks?

W.R. Cooke: No, it's a knife. Here, I'll show you. (Click, click) Here, I'm a little high... I can't do it right now.

McGrath: Wow, just what I need. A blade.

W.R. Cooke: I'll tell you why, man... I had a guy pull a fucking straight razor on me and my old lady once...

Mitch Ryder: Would you hand me that jacket right there? Billy, you just dropped the hash, right?

McGrath: Most groups that come to Vancouver usually... well, remark how much of a good time they had.

Mitch Ryder: It's got a nice image, you know. Like even in the States no matter where we go they say when we're going to Vancouver, "Oh man, it's so beautiful up there".

Bret Tuggle (guitar): People here are really strange. Only because they seem a little bit more inward than outward—even the freaks. Maybe that's just the way things are here. Kinda quiet and like—but when they get down to some music—they're not cold or anything. Maybe just suspicious. Maybe it's because we're Americans or maybe it's our group image. Like, I've gotten harassed least of all here than anywhere else, man. Like you can go down any major city, well, especially a small city, but like a major city where most of the people have already been through this trip. It seems that they would get used to it— that there's freaks in the world, man, and that they're gonna be there and that they got their own culture—they're gonna be there for a long time, and that they're gonna build it into a lasting culture—so like when you walk down the street there's still people freaking out—"Oh, look at that longhair—ugh—animal."

Mitch Ryder: They're probably thinking about their own children.

W.R. Cooke: Yeah, they probably are. Probably paranoid.

Harry Phillips: You guys from the city?

McGrath: Yeah... from the Georgia Straight.

W.R. Cooke: Oh, right. How long has that paper been in effect?

McGrath: Three years now.

W.R. Cooke: It's really doin' good from what I've heard. Got a couple of issues a week.

McGrath: Yeah, right.

W.R. Cooke: Fuck, that's bomber, man... couldn't ask for... that's killer, man... ain't no magazines in the world.
Ryder: What's this fixation you have with John Sinclair?

Sorensen: I met him once in Seattle, and I saw MC5 play.

Mitch Ryder: Had you corresponded with him?

Harry Phillips: Shoot away. Whatever you wanna know, man, about Billy or what... I'll tell you about him.

Mitch Ryder: You don't need to spill no beans like that. Let's find out if these guys are commie perverts first.

Sorensen: We did a benefit for John Sinclair.

Ryder: Oh, you did. We've done four or five.

KIM SIMMONDS: BLUES THINGS

Kerrisdale Arena, Vancouver, September, 1970

THIS WAS AN ATROCIOUS night of music: Atomic Rooster, a brit Spinal Tap band led by the talented yet tortured Vincent Crane, the deadly boring Redbone, and Savoy Brown, the backup band for guitar hero Kim Simmonds. After the concert I talked briefly with Crane, who didn't really want to chat, and then with the Savoy lead guitarist *par excellence*.

Simmonds was somewhat downbeat, despite his semi-optimistic answers. Understandable, actually, as Savoy Brown was a great rock/blues band before Simmonds rather extensively changed their style and personnel. This, in fact, was one of their last tours as Savoy Brown.

Rick McGrath: Perhaps the first thing we can talk about is your new album, Looking In.

Kim Simmonds: It's a lot different from our last albums, it's got a lot more influences outside the blues. Like, for instance, there's a couple of tracks with harmonies on them, which we've never tried before.

It's a most satisfying album for me, because we just went in there and played what we played without manufacturing any sounds, which means that we can go on stage and play the same thing. It's more real.

In the past we've gone into a studio and put horns on things, manufactured sounds which weren't quite what we were

on stage, which always pissed me off, you know? With this band here, well, what I like about it is that it's real.

McGrath: You've changed Savoy Brown since you were here last.

Kim Simmonds: I changed the band. The band that last played here was like a changed thing, and it just wasn't working out. I made a mistake there, I got some wrong fellows and they couldn't do the tunes, so I got rid of them and got some new people. You have just got to get the right people that you can work with.

McGrath: How's the tour going?

Kim Simmonds: Excellent so far. This is our second week. All the gigs have been really great so far.

McGrath: So you haven't been here long. What's happening in England these days?

Kim Simmonds: It depends what your taste is. Personally, in the music I like, and the music I like to play, England is dead. As far as R&B and blues go, there's very little market for it. But as far as Pop and general music go, it's a good scene.

McGrath: Can you explain the Black Sabbath thing?

Kim Simmonds: It's just a reaction against more serious type of things. You had the beginning of the underground, when there were bands that took things a little more seriously than previously.

Like getting into what they were playing and writing songs, and the people that listened to it were into it, but now there's a younger generation that have moved up that don't particularly want to hear sophisticated stuff.

They want to have a good time and Black Sabbath gives it to them. I think it's valid in that respect, in so far as there's a market for it, so it must be valid.

McGrath: Any fears about the blues revival dying out in North America?

Kim Simmonds: Yeah, well, the blues thing is going down rapidly. It's rapidly declined in England. There's still a lot of enthusiasts for it, but the enthusiasts tend to buy black records instead of white records. And it's difficult, really, to get them to understand that white music can be as valid as black music.

Like, I still buy Paul Butterfield records. There are still guys around playing the blues, and there are still people digging it.

Gordon Lightfoot: Whiskey & Pretzels

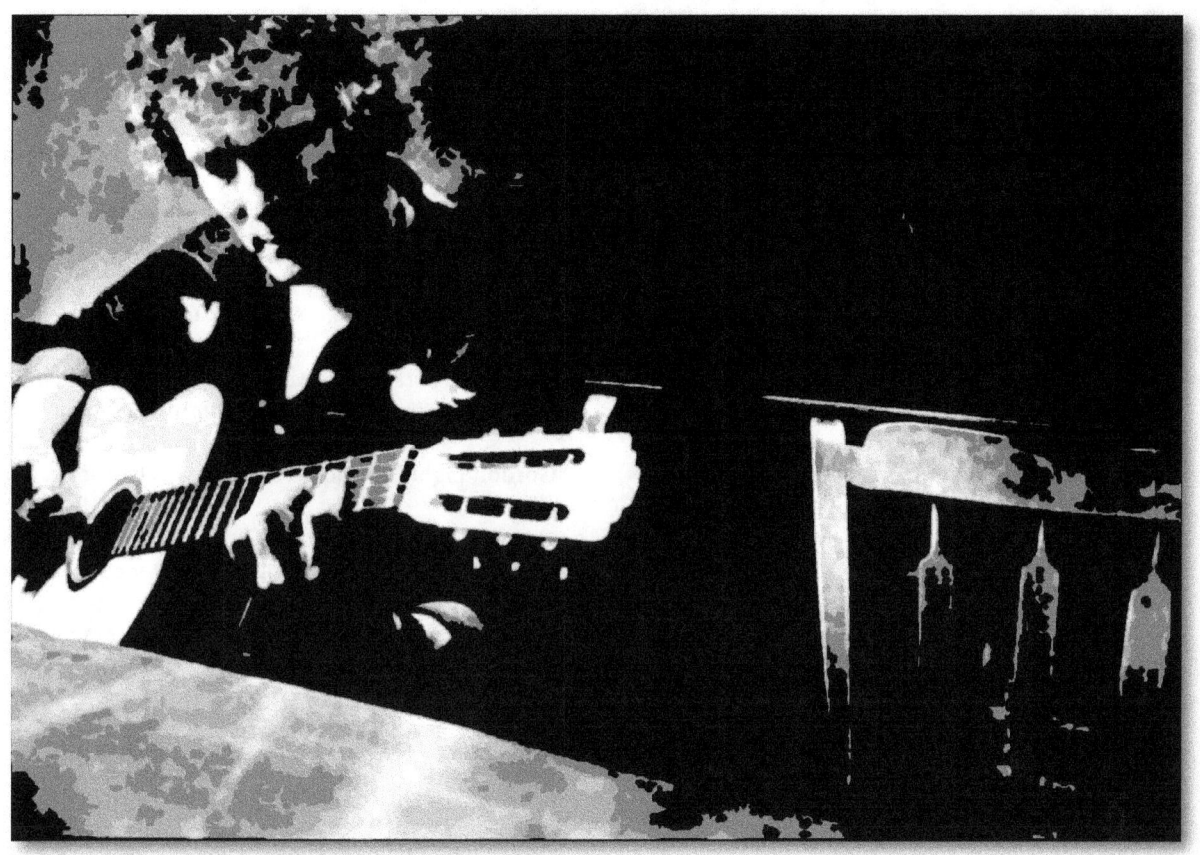

Bayshore Inn, Vancouver, October, 1970.

ANOTHER ASSIGNMENT with *Georgia Straight* classical music critic Mike Quigley. We made it to the Bayshore Inn on time for the interview, but soon found out that things were running a little late. Lightfoot was still with a man from CBC Radio, so we had to wait.

And wait.

Lounging in the Bayshore lobby is a strange experience in itself, but this time the whole thing seemed even more absurd. As the palace of choice for touring rockers with big budgets and bad taste—OK, it did have a great swimming pool and was close to venues—the Bayshore was a tad incongruous for two hairy guys dressed in radical chic. Finally our turn came, and we were ushered into the iconic Gordon Lightfoot's presence. The singer was wearing his TV togs: a jean suit with the jacket bespeckled with flying birds and symbolic sunsets. He wasn't too happy to talk to *The Straight*, presumably because we had half-panned his last album. But hell, man, he was still a folkie doing acoustic stuff in 1970.

We were digging LedZep. Gord's big electric hits, *The Wreck of the Edmund Fitzgerald* and *Sundown* were released four and six years later. So the whole conversation was a bit strained at first, but he opened up after a while and we had some fun.

Gordon Lightfoot: OK, what are we going to start off with?

Mike Quigley: You switched from BMI to ASCAP recently, didn't you?

Gordon Lightfoot: I switched from ASCAP to CAPAC.

Rick McGrath: Oh, and what were the reasons for that?

Gordon Lightfoot: No reason at all. It was a gesture of Canadianism. Actually, they've chased me around for quite some time to see if I would join the Canadian Songwriters' Society, and I was a member of the American one, and so finally after about two years I said OK, so give me the goddamn papers and I'll join CAPAC. I don't know why I did it, I have no reason whatsoever.

Quigley: There's no difference in the way they handle your royalties and things like that?

Gordon Lightfoot: I don't know a thing about it, I'm not into finances. I'm not even interested in money. As a matter of fact probably my income tax supports a lot of people in this country.

McGrath: What are your political views about what happens in this country?

Gordon Lightfoot: I find it totally unpredictable. I know that we're being inexorably taken over by the Americans. Without a doubt. I don't mean invaded or anything like that, just taken over. By degrees.

(long pause)

McGrath: On that happy note...

Gordon Lightfoot: Wait till I get some cheese (stands and walks over to a snack-covered table).

Bruce Bissell (Warner Promo Man): You guys sure have rhythm.

Quigley: You sit down in the Bayshore lobby for an hour...

Gordon Lightfoot: Did we keep you waiting?

McGrath: Sitting down there eating a hamburger and listening to stereo muzak is not my idea of paradise.

Gordon Lightfoot: I know what you mean, I've lived in hotels for years.

Quigley: How many interviews have you had today?

Gordon Lightfoot: Two straight and one freak-out.

Quigley: Which one was that?

Gordon Lightfoot: The guy from CBC Radio (laughs).

McGrath: How do you like doing all of them in a row?

Gordon Lightfoot: Well, my throat hurts. I should be in bed. I've been boogeyin' all night long. And I had to get up to get down here and I want to be back in bed by three.

McGrath: So what have you got next in the way of records? (laughs) How many times have you been asked that question? (adopts deep FM voice) Gordon, what's your next record going to be?

Lightfoot turns slightly to his side and farts loudly into the microphone. Much laughter, etc.

McGrath: Is that a critical opinion?

Gordon Lightfoot: That's a political opinion.

Quigley: What's this 25 verse song that you're doing now. They mentioned it in Canadian Composer. Will it be on the next album?

Gordon Lightfoot: No. I'd never record that song. (pause)

Quigley: Just to fill the listeners in on what's not happening, Gordon Lightfoot, could you perhaps tell us what the song is about?

Gordon Lightfoot: Do I have to? I mean, after all, it is 25 verses long. I could be here all day.

McGrath: In ten words or less what is the general theme of the composition, perhaps? Is it Canadian nationalism stuff like the Great Train Robbery trilogy? Pollution? Ecology?

Gordon Lightfoot: No, it's not one of those. *The Great Train Robbery* trilogy? No.

McGrath: Do you still think of yourself in any way as a Canadian writer?

Gordon Lightfoot: Yes, I think so. I am a Canadian.

McGrath: Do you get your material from Canadian situations?

Gordon Lightfoot: No, I get them from life in general I believe. I mean I consider myself to be a part of the overall music scene. I don't have any hangups about Canadians being oppressed and talent being held down. The only problem we have here is an enormous influence from the USA on all sides. And how can you fight against that kind of strength? I mean—well, let me be more explicit: you have a 4500 mile border and it goes alongside the most powerful country on earth. They're putting out this mass of product, which also includes the music bag. So they're beaming in across the border with their radio stations and everything, so how are you going to fight that. So it gives Canadians a complex to have that happening, not only in the music business, but all business in Canada. We're very heavily influenced.

Quigley: What do you think about the new 30% Canadian content regulations? Someone said it was going to bring out a lot of junk.

Gordon Lightfoot: I don't think they should regulate the music field. I don't see how they can regulate the arts.

McGrath: They're doing it.

Gordon Lightfoot: I don't know, I just don't know what to make of it. It happened, I don't know anything about it, all I know it's a new rule for 30% Canadian product. I guess it's good. It's definitely going to influence the music industry. There will probably be some new studios built...

Quigley: There's lots of opportunities. We'd like to see a distinctive Canadian thing happen, and get away from this join the American industry to make money trip. It seems like if you want to make money and be famous you have to go to the states.

Gordon Lightfoot: Not necessarily.

McGrath: Well, who of any artistic repute hasn't?

Gordon Lightfoot: Not me.

McGrath: But you're on an American label.

Gordon Lightfoot: Yeah, but...

Quigley: Did you do your recording on your earlier albums in Canada, or was it done in the states?

Gordon Lightfoot: Some of it was done in the states—some in New York, some in Nashville, some in LA.

McGrath: Are there were no good studios in Canada?

Gordon Lightfoot: No, it was a matter of convenience. In other words, a producer has to drive through forty minutes of downtown New York traffic and I have to put four guys on a plane and fly 500 miles. I guess he figured it was more convenient for us. It's a matter of wherever it's right for everyone to get together and get it done. I did one session while I was in Nashville doing the Johnny Cash show.

Quigley: Have you done any more TV shows?

Gordon Lightfoot: CTV, *Nashville North*, *David Frost*, oh, that was a bummer.

Quigley: Are you pretold what the questions are, or is it really spontaneous?

Gordon Lightfoot: Not only was I not told what the questions were going to be, I was lucky to get on. They cut me off in the middle of my second song with the end of the show. I'll never go near the bugger again. Well, I guess it's his producer that's to blame. And then there was Carol Channing yapping away and George Jessel and you can't shut them up.

I was hoping to get on and get rolling and they'd let me keep going, like he did some of the other guys. And we were sitting around all day, we had a list of songs all ready to go in rapid fire—we were really going to get rolling and he'd love every song and he'd say sing another one and sing another...

And all of a sudden it came up to the last five minutes of the show and we were starting to wonder if we were going to get on and then all of a sudden this silly-ass producer comes running out and says you gotta change your last song, have you got something shorter for your second song. So there we were in a complete dither. And we went on and I launched into *Early Mornin' Rain* and he came running over and said "Did you write that?" and I felt like saying "Of course I wrote it" and he said "Do you write all your own songs?" and then he said "Well, give us another quickie," so I launched into *Saturday Clothes* and they cut me off right in the middle of it. All of a sudden everyone started yelling and I was still singing and the show was over. And the applause sign was flashing on and off and it was a nightmare.

So we went out and in order to make the thing I had to hire a private plane to get us up to Toronto and it cost something like $680 to fly up in a Grand Commander from New York to Toronto at one o'clock in the morning and there were no peanuts left because Sly and the Family Stone cleaned the cat out the night before, so we didn't have any peanuts. All we had was a bottle of whiskey and some pretzels.

McGrath: Sounds like great lyrics for a song.

Van Morrison: Astral Breakfast

Vancouver International Airport, February 3, 1971

VAN THE MAN! For me, this was a long time coming—I had been a fan since 1965, when *Gloria* first hit the airwaves and I rushed out to buy that incendiary first *Them* album. Couldn't get enough of that Belfast Blues with the scruffy band and the obviously intense little red-haired lead singer who could belt it out with an almost obsessive intensity.

Getting this interview wasn't easy. Van didn't like the press much—remember, this was 1971, only a couple of years after he was vilified for alleged drug use—and his prior life as a top 40 hitman. It was set up at the Vancouver airport the morning after the show, and I think for all of us it was a different gig: I'd never interviewed a rock star over bacon and eggs, and I doubt if Van had much of a conception of what an underground newspaper was all about…

Regardless, he seemed to enjoy himself; we laughed a lot, and members of the band listened in and made a few comments, as well.

Rick McGrath: To get things started. What were your feelings about the Vancouver show generally?

Van Morrison: I think it could have been better. Sound-wise it wasn't too good because we weren't hearing each other. Stuff like that.

And whoever was doing the lights didn't know what was happening because, you know, someone would take a solo and he would put the lights on the wrong cat, stuff like that. The guy with the lights didn't have an ear for music, and so that part of it was all—*pshew*—the lights were up in the air.

The sound wasn't too good.

McGrath: You usually travel with the Street Choir—Janet Planet, Martha Velez and Ellen Schroer. But they weren't here this time.

Van Morrison: They only come with us in situations where we can all travel comfortably. This one happens to be a haphazard tour.

McGrath: I've heard albums by Martha Velez on her own. How did you pick up on her?

Van Morrison: The trumpet player, Keith Johnson, she's married to him. All I remember is just one night she was there, that's all I remember.

McGrath: She's got a fine voice.

Van Morrison: Yeah.

McGrath: You guys are a great band. How did you get together?

John Platania (lead guitar): I just came in and played.

McGrath: This next question is sort of in response to the review of your show in the local dailies, both of which emphasized the point that your stage presence was less than exciting. I would like to know if you are self conscious about your stage presence at all.

Van Morrison: Is this tape on?

McGrath: Yes.

Van Morrison: You wouldn't know it (laughs). Go ahead.

McGrath: Are you aware of your actions onstage?

Van Morrison: It's a lot of things. It's like, I mean, when you have to get up and travel for like six or seven hours and stuff like that. Personally, I can't really perform my best under those conditions. I can't really do it as well as I could because you're tired when you get there. It's hard to explain. I can only get really into it when I'm comfortable.

McGrath: What I was wondering, though, was when you get onstage do you have an action plan of some sort?

Van Morrison: We plan most of our set; sometimes we change it when we're on. We know what we're doing when we're on.

McGrath: You don't perform the songs live the same as the album—is this on purpose?

Van Morrison: I seldom play the same thing twice. If we do play the same thing twice I usually say "why?"

McGrath: I was thinking about how the audience can be a drain on the performer creatively.

Van Morrison: Yeah, right.

McGrath: The audience can often control a performer like a puppet. I think something like that is really damaging to an artist.

Van Morrison: Yeah, it's a drag. Most of the audience has a set thing and before they come they have a set thing about the performer from radio and record exposure. Then they expect a certain thing and when they don't get exactly what they expect, it throws them off balance.

McGrath: What I don't think the audience understands is that the recording is a real artificial representation of the artist. The artist, when he records, is at the mercy of an engineer and a vast array of gadgets.

Van Morrison: Right.

McGrath: And the finished product may not be the way the artist intended.

Van Morrison: Dig it. Perhaps the truest way you can come to any kind of real recording is doing it live, you know, you just go in and do the songs live without any overdubbing and get it within the first two or three takes. That's where it's really true to what you're doing. When you do a thing and mix it then it becomes something else, a production.

McGrath: I notice this same thing happening in the album—a progression from Astral Weeks to Domino. Things are getting looser. Are you planning this into the albums?

Van Morrison: We always try and get that. It all depends on the circumstances. Sometimes you can get it, sometimes you can't. It all depends on your day, or like who's doing what, or what engineer you've got. It's got to do with a lot of things.

McGrath: When you go into the studio, do you go in with a pretty sure idea of what you want the song to sound like, or do you work it out in the studio?

Van Morrison: Sometimes, like on the last album, songs were just done in the studio. I just called the numbers and we did

them for the first time in the studio. But others we work out before we go in.

McGrath: It's been two years since Astral Weeks has been released, and it was preceded by about two years of silence.

Van Morrison: How do you mean silence?

McGrath: Well, "Brown Eyed Girl" was released in 1967, and that was it until 1969.

Van Morrison: I was still recording.

McGrath: What happened to that stuff?

Van Morrison: I've got some of it (laughs).

McGrath: It wasn't released on records at all.

Van Morrison: No, it wasn't released.

McGrath: That's what I mean by silence.

Van Morrison: Oh, well, just because you don't have a record out—that doesn't have anything to do with anything. It really doesn't have much to do with music, whether you've got a record out or not.

McGrath: But as far as the public is concerned, there's a big gap between Brown Eyed Girl and Astral Weeks.

Van Morrison: Are you talking about it like in terms of hit singles or something?

McGrath: No, in terms of progression. Like, you're going to keep on progressing as a musician, changing and evolving, but the public. I was not aware of what you were doing during those two years.

Van Morrison: That's another story. I don't even know what it is. It's beyond my imagination what that is. The system or the press or whatever. I don't know what that is. It doesn't have anything to do with me. I don't think you can really generalize about what the public sees and what you're doing. Because what the public sees and what you're doing are just different. The public doesn't see you all the time, so they've just got to go on what they can get. It's a very artificial way of doing it.

McGrath: Especially when one realizes that the artist must keep changing.

Van Morrison: I do other things than playing music. I do a lot of other things rather than that. It probably isn't a big part of my life. It's just a small part. I think that's why. I mean, I don't know anything about the Beatles, but it always struck me about the Beatles that everyone had this thing in their head about the Beatles and they wouldn't accept anything else. Even if one of the Beatles said, "Here's where we're really at—blah, blah blah." They wouldn't accept it because it would ruin the image, or something like that. That's nonsense. How can you base your life on that? Some kind of image.

McGrath: It's like you spend your public moments pretending to be someone else.

Van Morrison: Sometimes, it's not them. They probably didn't have any say about it—I don't know, but a lot of people don't have any say about what they're surrounded with. Like something's promoted a certain way. You could be totally different and be promoted as something else. People show up and they say, "Well, we saw this ad in a paper saying you were going to act like this or sing like this and that's something else." That's like on the other side of the tracks.

McGrath: Do you find this happens to you?

Van Morrison: Not any more (laughs). I don't think it happens any more.

McGrath: But it did at one time?

Van Morrison: Yeah, one time it did.

McGrath: Musically, you seem to be getting back to R&B. Or is that an assumption on my part?

Van Morrison: I think it's an assumption. Personally, I play a lot of different kinds of music and I enjoy playing them all. I'm not getting back to one thing.

McGrath: But your last two albums have been predominantly R&B and during the concert the songs you did do off Astral Weeks were changed so that they seemed to be like the more recent stuff. What about that?

Van Morrison: I really don't know what to say (laughs).

Jack Schroer (Saxophone): Did you really expect the *Astral Weeks* songs to be the same?

McGrath: No, I wasn't expecting them to be the same. It's an entirely different band, so the sound will change. Might we assume the way you perform songs is a reflection of your current musical interests?

Van Morrison: Oh, a lot of jazz, folk, blues, R&B, pop, rock, classical. I like a lot of things. I'm into a lot of different kinds of music. I couldn't really say, "This is where it's at… this is what I think."

McGrath: I think what we've been talking about would really shock the average fan, who expects an artist to cut an album, get out there, and recite the album like somebody had turned a key in his back. This is so wrong. Like the story about Phil Spector asking you about the "true meaning" of your songs.

Van Morrison: You heard about that? It was sick. I saw a program on TV last night about Newton. And these two guys were dissecting him piece by piece. All his ideas, and what do they know? They're sitting there, talking about something that they're wasting their time on. Newton just did what he did.

McGrath: John Mayall once gave me some pretty good advice on the whole criticism thing. The safest way to do it, he said, was to just sit down with the person who made the album and rap about it. The next best thing is to sit down and just expand on the images that come from the music. This is fine, as long as the people who we're writing for realize that what we write is just one man's opinion, and that everyone gets different images.

Van Morrison: Right.

McGrath: Like a free association thing.

Van Morrison: Yeah. It's going to be one fellow's opinion, because it's going to mean something different to everybody. But I think that someone in your position could influence someone by writing, say, "I think this means that." A lot of people would read that and probably take that and say, "Well, he thinks that and he's a writer so… and I'm sitting reading this paper so that must be where it's at." Yeah?

McGrath: Yeah. A lot of people might not want to buy a record just to see if they like it, so they read about it.

Van Morrison: That could be a groovy way of stimulation. Somebody's got to do it because if somebody didn't do it then a lot of people wouldn't be stimulated at all to think about anything.

Dahaud Shaar (drummer): Most people, too, really want to know. A person reading a paper really wants to know if this album is good or bad.

Van Morrison: It's like I used to get these magazines, *Jazz Journal*. They used to be the English equivalent of *Downbeat*. And all these guys used to review all the albums and I used to read the reviews and then sometimes I'd listen to the album and

say "What?" because they just reviewed the album the way they were feeling.

If they weren't feeling good that day they'd say "This album sucks," but if they were feeling all right, the album would be groovy. That kind of thing, you just can't go on that.

McGrath: How do you feel about interviews? I can imagine everybody and his dog sticking a mike in your face and asking things like "What's your favorite color, Van?"... How do you feel, as an artist, when you read things written about you?

Van Morrison: What's my reaction? A lot of times I feel like the cat was right there, he was tight with it and he knew what was happening and he was tuned in. Many times I feel that a lot of people just turn themselves off, and see it from a long way off. They put a barrier between themselves and the music, and they write about it like that.

I think things are getting better, though. It seems things are starting to open up. People are starting to be truthful with one another about the whole thing.

McGrath: Yeah, like writers are starting to admit they aren't members of the thought police, and are saying instead this is what I feel about this record, or this concert. Like I feel Astral Weeks was really a concept album. I read somewhere you thought it might be a rock opera.

Van Morrison: That all depends on what you mean by rock. A lot of people, when you say rock think of, say, The Doors. A lot of people think of something else. I wouldn't really say it was a rock opera. It's definitely an opera. There's more to it than the album. The album's just a piece of it. There's a whole lot more stuff that I've got.

McGrath: It's got a definite story line.

Van Morrison: Oh yeah, there's a definite story and it all fits together. Just by the fact that it's one album with a minimum 38 minutes. You can't really get into it in 38 minutes. Plus the way the album was done I didn't get a chance to get into it either. Because my producer told me you've got so much time to finish this album and you've got to go in and do it. So I booked the time and that was it. I only got that time.

And I didn't really get into it as much as I thought I would because of that. Because you lease out these sessions, about six sessions, and that's all the time I had. They said "You've got to do it within this time," whereas if I had my way it would have been a different thing.

McGrath: I noticed on Astral Weeks that some of the songs and some of the images seem to have been carried on from your earlier work. Cypress Avenue, for instance, has a lot in common with Little Girl from your Here Comes the Night album.

Van Morrison: Yeah, it's a similar thing.

McGrath: I listened to the albums for awhile, and then I started to realize there seemed to be some kind of story evolving from the earlier stuff. That you were taking personal experiences and writing about them...

Van Morrison: Right, yeah.

McGrath: And that's what I really got into, that's what I really dug, is that it wasn't just an imagination trip...

Van Morrison: No.

McGrath: There was some honesty to it, some reality.

Van Morrison: Yeah.

Fleetwood Mac: Jeremy Spencer's Last Interview

Bayshore Inn, Vancouver, February 10, 1971

I REMEMBER this one very well. The night of the unknown Mac. As you can see from the promo poster, Christine Perfect had just joined the group, replacing the genius bluesman, Peter Green.

Nine days after this interview Jeremy Spencer would leave the group in Los Angeles to join the Children Of God cult. Peter Green rejoined the group briefly so they could finish the tour, but Jeremy would finally be replaced by Bob Welsh, who hung around for five albums before going off on his own trip. A couple of years later, Mick meets two kids from L.A. and invites them to join the band... and the rest is...

Rick McGrath: You people have moved to a farm?

Mick Fleetwood: It's not a farm, it's just a big house.

McGrath: And it has a studio?

Mick Fleetwood: Yeah, I think by the time we get back to London it will be a four-track setup, but it will be eight-track shortly afterwards. It's supposed to be eight-track, but they've still got to get hold of the heads and everything. We've done things just on normal tape recorders that would have been, with a little more care, feasible, perfectly all right. So four tracks is plenty to start with. I don't think, unless you're really planning to do huge things with synthesizers, eight-track is perfect. Sixteen track I don't think we'll ever use.

McGrath: Do you see this set-up working as a Beatles or Chicago thing?

Mick Fleetwood: I think the idea appeals to us, to be able to do that. Initially the setup is for us, but I think if the opportunity came along where someone wasn't fortunate enough to be able to afford studio prices, which a lot of groups can't, because they don't have a good record deal or something, then obviously I think we'd very much like to do that—record them. I think, really, it's something like that.

I think it's a good idea to have somebody build a studio, not in a private house like ours, but right in the country with very pleasant surroundings where a group can actually go out for a fortnight and live in the studio… live there, sleep there.

McGrath: When you record, do you work things out in the studio at all?

Mick Fleetwood: It has worked like that. We have done that where Danny has worked something out or when Peter was in the band, he used to work things out and, even to the extent where he used to lay a lot of the tracks down himself, you know, just go in and use the tracks. But as a rule, I'd say no, things are not super worked out. I know some bands do that.

McGrath: What I'm leading up to is the problem of spontaneity in the studio. Even though you overdub, do you try and get things down in as few takes as possible?

Mick Fleetwood: All the time. You've definitely got it in the back of your head that the least amount of time is that you have to do it. Obviously if someone goofs up or something you've got to do it again because it just isn't right, but I think that's right, especially with singing.

If you find that you're singing it time and time again, you should either leave it completely, or if you're not getting something going the way you know it should be, and you know it's wrong, you can get to a stage where you should just leave it for a week, and go in fresh.

Because it is a bad thing to overdo it.

McGrath: Will your new album be like Kiln House?

Jeremy Spencer: No, Chris will be on it for a start. It will have the same sort of sound, even more normal and more natural. The influences are still the same.

McGrath: Where did you pick up the Blue Suede Shoes thing? Like the movements and stuff?

Jeremy Spencer: I just started in my front room playing around with an old guitar and picked it up from there. I copied the movements from old photographs. Not moving photographs, but old stills. It was just fun. I suppose every kid used to do that.

McGrath: It is really effective. There seems to be a lot of old Rock doing a revival thing these days, what with Sha Na Na and Brownsville Station. Do you parody the old days, or are you really into it?

Jeremy Spencer: You've got to parody it a little bit, but I mean I really like it and I listen to it a lot.

McGrath: Are you going to be incorporating anymore of it into your act?

Jeremy Spencer: For the next album?

McGrath: Either for live shows or an album.

Jeremy Spencer: Oh yeah. The reason it was like that on *Kiln House* is because we had to do an album in two weeks.

McGrath: Did you find that difficult to do?

Mick Fleetwood: Yeah, the whole band was in a bit of a turmoil. First of all we hadn't fulfilled our contract in making another American tour. We had to do two every year. And we had to make another record. We have to do three albums a year, and we hadn't done either of those, so we had to do one to tie in with the American tour, which isn't unreasonable at all. I mean the point is, had we not done *Kiln House*, we still wouldn't have had an album out now. So really, there was that reason too, but the really big reason that it was quite important that the band put out something.

I mean, that was an honest thing to do. It's not something we would say "awww" to, it wasn't perhaps everything it could have been, like there wasn't much thought attached to it, in the way that you were saying, like "Do you think about it?" which, obviously, I think you should. Think about the basic format that you're going to present. Well, there wasn't much of that involved.

It was just a case of really doing it, and getting into the studio and making an album. And that was it. And that's the circumstances. Chris wasn't on it, but she's in the band now, you see, so the band still hasn't got, hasn't presented anything that is really from the band. Wholly, as a unit.

McGrath: And the next one will, and you'll have the time to do it.

Mick Fleetwood: It certainly won't happen again. But we certainly don't regret it. There were certain circumstances that were certainly not the best to make an album under.

McGrath: It's rather surprising to me that the disc turned out as fine as it did, what with all these problems. It's a fine album. When you do a live show, do you find the audience demands change very much of your set? That is, do you find yourself getting into a rut by having to play the oldies?

Mick Fleetwood: I don't think as a band we do that very much. For instance, we don't play anything off *Then Play On*, or something like that. When we last came to America this album, *Kiln House*, wasn't out. It came out when we left. So you can imagine. Peter had just left the band, Christine had joined about four days before, and added to that we didn't play, we just did not play, anything that was familiar with what they'd heard before, so, I mean, there was a large chunk of well-known numbers that Peter used to do and we just didn't do them, so I mean, someway or another, you could have done them but it would have been a little funny doing them because you'd think we had to.

I mean, a lot of people probably didn't know that Peter Green had left the band, and then we turn up with a girl that's doing material she had never heard before, because the album wasn't out, so it must have been pretty weird.

McGrath: It was a bit unexpected. The reviewers for the other papers got everything screwed up. They thought Jeremy was Peter and they didn't know who the hell Christine was. That may explain the rather lame reviews, because how can you remain credible when you don't even know who you're writing about. Is Christine around? John?

Mick Fleetwood: She's out with John, probably shopping.

McGrath: That sounds fairly domestic.

Mick Fleetwood: You never know. Maybe they're looking for a spare kidney.

McGrath: Huh?

Mick Fleetwood: John's missing one. Didn't you know that?

McGrath: Ahh, no. (we laugh) There's a bit of trivia! I can suggest some good hospital gift shops. To change the subject a bit—OK a lot, do you think the blues revival is still as big in England?

Jeremy Spencer: No, no. The bands that just play blues these days don't seem to be doing anything. It's just not being played right. I mean, if it's being played well, I'm sure the people would like it.

McGrath: Peter's new album, have you heard it?

Mick Fleetwood: It's a jam.

McGrath: Yeah, the whole thing.

Mick Fleetwood: It's not a bad jam, though

McGrath: Yeah, but jams are pretty limited. You have to have more than one imagination working.

Mick Fleetwood: They're not sparking off properly.

McGrath: There are a couple cuts that are highly suggestive, but there's a few that don't do anything for me.

Jeremy Spencer: As far as playing the guitar, Peter is good, and some of the cuts sound like wild animals.

McGrath: Yeah, especially the first cut. And it's done with a wah-wah

Mick Fleetwood: The whole thing is wah-wah, isn't it?

Jeremy Spencer: Yeah, it seems that wah-wahs aren't very popular these days.

Mick Fleetwood: Well, Jimi Hendrix played it so well that I thought people were scared to use it after him because he played it the best. If you're not going to do anything different, what's the point?

McGrath: What do you think about the music scene?

Mick Fleetwood: The record business is fucking up the whole scene. There should be more free music. I think the people are putting too much responsibility on the bands for charging too much. And it's got nothing to do with them. Think of all the bands that charge exorbitant fees.

Kelly Jay: Lurking With Lennon

Bayshore Inn, Vancouver, March 10, 1971.

HERE'S THE FIRST of two interviews I did with Kelly Jay, the pianist and singer for Crowbar, one of the best of Canada's rock groups to spring up out of the wilds of the Ontario hinterland. I'm talking Hamilton.

Kelly, who must have set a new promotion endurance record in Vancouver, is, as you'll discover, one of the more outspoken rockers around.

Kelly really raps, and that's all there is to it.

Rick McGrath: I heard you know John Lennon. How is that?

Kelly Jay: I've been waiting for someone to ask me that. Thanks very much. We met John Lennon at Ronnie Hawkins' farm, right, when he came for the *Peace Festival*. And we were there with him and we saw the whole superstar thing. My first contact with someone like Lennon.

We walked into Hawkins' farm, and he was on one of those snowmobile things. And he was driving around and I came up from behind a bush and I figured I'd really play a number on him. I figured there was really only one way to meet this cat and that's to totally just do a number all over him when you first meet him, cause it's the only way you're going to impress him, right? Not "impress" him, you know, but I figured this guy meets so many people that saying "Hi, I really dug your record" isn't going to cut it.

So, it was when those laugh bags first came out, and we had six of them, so I took one and we all signed it "To John Lennon from The Hawks." So I stepped out from behind this bush—I was wearing this long velvet cape, so I put it over my head (I still had my frisbee, a fantastic afro)—with this bag laughing, and I said, "Take this, man, and may it serve you well," and he said, "Oh, what's this?" and I walked away and he just sat there, man, just sitting on the machine, and he was literally cracking up, he just dug the thing so much.

He came into the house afterwards and he sat down and we were rapping with him and we said we had our instruments set up at *Old Yeller* (Ronnie Hawkins' rehearsal barn) so why don't you come over and jam with us? And he says, "Oh no" and we say "OK, that's cool." So we went and rehearsed and he came over to the door of the house, and he was gonna come in, then he came in and listened, and he was getting a little closer and he wanted to play, and just as he was going to some other people showed up at the house and then Lennon said no because he felt he was being manoeuvred into jamming with us.

Like, what the fuck do we care? I mean it would have been really a gas to jam with John Lennon but I've jammed with Johnny Winter and Otis Spann. And Otis died a week later. So then Lennon's into all this neurosis shit and how he hates to be manoeuvred into things. He figured he was being jived into playing. Which is a bunch of horseshit, because we asked him if he wanted to, and we told him it was cool, because we were going to jam anyway. So there's this thing, right? He asked for all the shit he got, as far as I'm concerned. You read his interview in *Rolling Stone*? He just ripped off everybody in the group, which is totally unfair. We sat down and made credits and debits of who did what on the albums and we added them up. Like ripping off that side of *Abbey Road*, did you really think that was fair? Which side did you like?

McGrath: I like side two best.

Kelly Jay: That's the side that he really super ripped off. Like, *Oh Darling* was pretty good, but it certainly wasn't a landmark in rock'n'roll. He starts laying down all this shit about how he did this and that and he completely forgets about McCartney and Harrison.

McGrath: He seems to be really ticked off with McCartney's, but that could be a reaction because they were so close for so long.

Kelly Jay: Then I have something that's completely on the other side of that whole thing, that my interminable faith in The Beatles makes me want to believe this: that I think it's just a bunch of horseshit and that they're doing something and they're going to come back in a year and say "You see, all the world needs now is love. We really meant all that we said."

Like, that's going along with the myth, right? Like I really believe in the island of Greece, and I really believe there's phone numbers that you spell backwards, because there have been too many Beatle lies. There's been the thing about *Dr. Robert*.

McGrath: Here's another bit of Beatle myth: on the flip side of the single Let It Be there is a strange song, which, when played backwards, has John distinctly repeating, "Yes, I was the grandfather of them all" about five times. Very distinct.

Kelly Jay: What's the name of that song?

McGrath: It's called You Know My Name (Look Up the Number).

Kelly Jay: I gotta try that. You see, the reason why I believe this is because for 10 years people were allowed to believe that myth. Then all of a sudden it became very unhip to believe that myth and it became funny to believe in it.

And it seems like the truths that people once held have become plastic and immature. But good, honest, straight values don't change overnight, man.

If that (makes peace sign) represents peace and peace means people living together in harmony then how can something like that go out of fad?

McGrath: I think it has a lot to do with cynicism. So many people used these things to their own ends, be it power or money, that the truth of the gesture was lost.

Kelly Jay: That's true, man, but you can't give up just because a few people use things for themselves. But at any rate I believe that The Beatles are going to come back, but in the meantime, I'm going to go along with this thing, that if that's what it is, then I'll say right now that John Lennon is one of the finest actors in history, cause he's finally come out and said, "OK, you didn't like it when I came out and said I was bigger than Jesus… you didn't accept that, you don't believe it when we told you things in our songs that we had put some thought behind, so we'll just have to show you." So then they go about creating this elaborate death thing and then the breakup, and all these things in a horseshit context of, like, publishing it in the biggest voice rock paper in the world, of this is how I feel. And everybody will believe it and then when that's over they'll come out and show us the horseshit of the whole thing.

McGrath: Yeah, I didn't really believe the interview at all. It seemed too sensationalistic, too forced, to be Lennon. And there were slight differences in Lennon's speaking style.

Kelly Jay: That's exactly it. It doesn't seem to be Lennon speaking. It's really freaky because you go, "No, it can't be true after all these years that I really dug this cat." I'll accept the fact that I could be wrong about Hawkins' party—I could have misinterpreted the whole thing—he might just have been tired, man, but I know he dug our group.

Maybe it was just me, being snotty or something, like I never really formed those opinions until after I read the *Rolling Stone* thing, and a few others, and I figured, shit, and I threw the paper down and I stomped on it and went out and broke the record. I don't like his new record.

McGrath: Can't you get off on the words, because if they're true, he's really laying a lot of it out bare.

Kelly Jay: Who cares? I don't care about his neuroses.

McGrath: Don't you think it's past that? I think he's verging on some kind of picture of the human condition. Finding about everything from a close examination of one thing.

Kelly Jay: Do you think that album is a criterion of the elevation of a human being? Do you think that's a plateau you would like to reach?

McGrath: I don't think that's the way you should react to the record.

Kelly Jay: Do you envy him for coming out and saying what he said in public?

McGrath: I think he's got a lot of guts, or else it's a big put-on to grab a certain market of the record-buying public who would dig that trip.

Kelly Jay: That's what I'm trying to get at. There's two sides to everything.

McGrath: Sounds like a record.

ELTON JOHN: THIS IS MY SONG

Vancouver, April, 1971

THIS INTERVIEW was different in the sense it was totally set up by Elton John's record company. They rented a big room, invited pretty well anybody remotely related to Vancouver's music scene and showered us with free drinks while Elton sat at a table and the assembled hordes got to take 15-minute turns with this surprisingly poppish little Brit, a bit of a twizzler, decked out in a frilly Tom Jones shirt, red Edwardian jacket—late mod?—complete with a Julius Caesar haircut and an incongruous Donald Duck button. And Brydsian glasses. An unusual look for 1971—or maybe not: one of Vancouver's big radio station moguls arrived for the event in an orange jumpsuit.

After we each had our speed date The EJ announces he'll play us a song and wanders off to a piano in the center of the room. Before you can say *I Need A Prop!* he's spotted an infant in the crowd. Before you can say *Photo Op!* he's grabbed the kid and plunked it on the piano and launches into an abridged version of *Your Song*, the big megahit from the *Friends* album. The crowd went wild. Well, let's say we were amused. And then off he went.

All in all, a slick, professional promotional event.

Mike Quigley and I did this gig together, and we were not too amused with this *flagrante* show of supreme flackery. Elton had even done some homework on us! Mike essentially said hello, and Elton started flattering him about one of his articles—be still, my fluttering heart!

What follows is a very revealing interview with a Man On The Way Up! Elton's early *Hi, how are ya* personality shines oh so brightly....

Mike Quigley: Welcome to Vancouver...

Elton John: I'm glad we got an opportunity to talk. I read your article last night, and I was very impressed by it. No, I really liked it—there was a review of *Friends* in *Rock Magazine* which took about twelve lines and really slated (sic) it, and it amused me—not amused me, but I'd quite like to meet the person who wrote that review and talk to him, because I get so bored with people saying, "Oh here we are: Wonder-Dog of 1971." The whole *Georgia Straight* magazine was quite interesting. I read a lot of that sort of thing. "Mikey Muzak" quite amused me. I actually heard *Your Song* on Muzak the other day and it freaked me out.

Rick McGrath: What do you think of all this (flack cocktail party routine).... doing this kind of stuff?

Elton John: I'm used to it, believe me. First time I came over to Los Angeles when it all sort of happened, as I said before I just met so many people like this—I'm immune to it now. I go through it all with a "Oh well, it must be done," and that's it. I really couldn't come down here and say "fuck off"—it's not me. I've been through this before—if I was a Mick Jagger person I'd just come down here and tell everyone to piss off, but that's not me. I can't do it. They're a necessary evil, I think.

Quigley: How much are we going to overlap here? What did you go through before?

Elton John: We went through a lot of things. It was quite good actually. I just said I wish somebody would attack me, as I thought you might be a good person to attack me.

Quigley: Why's that?

Elton John: Well, everyone's usually so nice to me. A young college kid came to New York when I was doing this college thing and he said "I think your music's rubbish," and I really appreciated that. We fought hammer and nail through the whole hour and a half that I spoke to him, and he ended up going out and buying a couple of my albums. No, it wasn't like that. (laughs)

People write about me in print but they never have the nerve to say it in front of my face. If they have any genuine feelings, they should tell me, because I respect their points of view.

Quigley: OK, on your latest album, which I reviewed this week...

Elton John: *Friends*. It's not my "latest album." It's a film soundtrack album which we contracted to do before *Elton John* was released. As a film soundtrack album, I think it's probably the best film soundtrack album ever released. Put that down in print.

McGrath: Do you think it represents you, though?

Elton John: Yes. No, it represents what we had to write for the film. The whole story behind the film was they contracted us to do three songs. There's a sequence in the film where they have a tape recorder sequence where everyone's leaping up and down for 20 seconds, and a radio sequence for 30 seconds, and they said "You're going to have to write two songs that last for 20 and 30 seconds, and put them on the album." I thought that was ridiculous. Bernie and I said "We can't do that," so they said, "We want three songs—one is the title song." And they wanted another song, which was to last a minute and ten. That was *Seasons*. And then they said "We want a soundtrack album," and I said "That's awful," because there's very little music in the film.

We knew we couldn't put an album together with just three songs on it. We said if we were going to do this thing with the 20 and 30 second songs, then we'll write two songs and re-record the whole album. So we recorded the whole album once for the film, and then went back into our studio and recorded the soundtrack album, just as a sort of—so people would at least get a bit of value for their money. They get five songs instead of three and bits of motorcars and horses galloping. It was recorded and written in four weeks—last September, and as a soundtrack album—I don't know—the record company are promoting it as a new Elton John album, and kids will probably think it is a new Elton John album.

Quigley: Especially since your name is bigger than the title of the film.

Elton John: Yeah, which is pissing me off somewhat. That's because the guy in London (who's a complete idiot) who runs Paramount Records, he wanted a good sleeve. So the people that produced the film took the *Tumbleweed Connection* up and said "Isn't this great? Look, it's got a booklet. We'd like something like this for *Friends*." And the guy said it was rubbish—the worst thing he'd ever seen, and he said "Wait till we come up—we'll come up with something that'll sweep this off the board." And they came up with that strawberry colored rubbish.

I suppose I can't blame the Paramount Record Company for putting my name on it in big letters, cause I would have probably done that—I don't know—I don't want to get into that anyway. It's not an *Elton John* album, believe me. The album was gold within three weeks, so that's amusing. I'm knocked out that it is gold. But it's not an *Elton John* album. We've got a live album coming out in three weeks.

McGrath: Somebody said you wanted it to be coupled with Empty Sky.

Elton John: Yeah, I did. I've had these hassles the past week. We've got two things which have been released in England which haven't been released here—*Empty Sky* and the live album, and I wanted *Empty Sky* and the live album to come out together for $5.98—because all my albums have gone up to $5.98, which I found out. So I wanted the live album to have a free album—you know, "Thank you very much, America... here's a free album—*Empty Sky*." And, of course, all the hierarchy that I'm concerned with said no. And I get so pissed off with fighting. Everyone had a different idea. They wanted the live album to come out in July, which would have been ludicrous, because so many people are importing it the album would have been dead. And other people wanted it not to come out at all (the live album). And some other people wanted *Empty Sky* to come out first. You wouldn't believe it. So we settled for *Empty Sky* not to come out yet, which is all right. They say that it's better for my "mystique" that it should remain on import. So that's the situation. I'm going to get criticized for the live album, because everyone will say, "Oh, fuck, not another Elton John album!" But it has to come out now, because it has been released and people are playing it. So I'm just going to have to face the criticism. It's a bloody good live album. What decided for me that it was a good live album was Crosby, Stills, Nash & Young, which I was eagerly awaiting, and I thought it was a total, utter disaster. I thought "Well we can't go much wrong than that. I hear that the CSN&Y live album is a gold record before it comes out. It's done two million dollars worth of sales. There's two or three really nice things on it, but I think it's an unmitigated disaster. I thought ours was so much better than that. It's not fair to point that out, but that's what decided that it really should come out.

McGrath: What do you think of the incredible amount of hype and mystique that's behind you? How do you relate to that?

Elton John: I know there's a lot of hype. I'm over in England so I'm not really aware. I have somebody who's trying to control it, one person. There's hype, but there's hype with everybody. It seems no matter what record company you're with, they're going to try to hype you, because, really, all record companies are interested in is making money. We have a very good relationship with MCA, a really fantastic relationship. I'd rather be hyped in the way I am than be hyped in the way that Warner-Reprise hype their artists. I think their ads are so hip they're revolting. And there's no new artists to break through on Warner Reprise Kinney Group Records, that I can think of in the last two or three years. I mean, they've just managed to break Gordon Lightfoot, which I thought was tremendous. I think that hype is more revolting. I'd rather have them saying "Here is the great Elton John—buy him!" than "Well, fellows—do a clever advert."

I'm not into that at all. It's just a snobbish way of saying "We're trying to be hip" and most of the people at Warner Brothers aren't hip. I really don't mind the hype. It's up to me to prove it, whether I'm worth it or not, or whatever it is. I mean, people have to decide for themselves. It's wrong for a person to decide that you're a hype just by listening to the adverts. They should go out and buy the records, discover whether you're a hype or not, or go and see you live. If then they've seen or heard you and they think you're a hype, then that's fair enough—they've had a chance to listen to you.

I don't think you can avoid it, can you? I mean, how can you possibly avoid being hyped? It's impossible. Some people don't get hyped enough, people like David Ackles, who could well be hyped as much as I've been. But once you're successful, they're going to try to get as much hype going as possible. And you have to live with that—it's a fact of life.

McGrath: Speaking about the music—with the last three albums we've noticed that the piano work and the melody line and the rhythm are starting to repeat themselves, and we were wondering if it's just because you happen to do these albums in a relatively short time.

Elton John: This is always amusing: "the melody line." Such as what? I mean, this guy in *Rock Magazine* said *Honey Roll* sounds like *Burn Down the Mission*, which I thought was vaguely amusing—the guy should be put into an institution.

Quigley: Well, you've got to admit that it's starting to—it might be because you've just got a heavily stylized way of playing and you pick it up really easily, therefore whenever you keep playing these things, the style comes out very predominantly. Your songs really remind me of each other.

Elton John: Well, all the new songs we've written are going to be on the next album. *Elton John, Tumbleweed Connection*, all the songs on them were written before the albums were recorded. I can see you repeat yourself, in a way. A lot of people. I suppose I always defend myself, it's pretty natural. I know what you mean about the beat, a lot of our songs.

McGrath: Like the dum-de-dum-de-dum (beginning of Your Song) riff happens a lot.

Elton John: Well, I like that. But you listen to a lot of Leon Russell's stuff, who's my idol, and I won't have a word said against him, a lot of his piano playing sounds. It's just a style you get into. I copied Leon Russell, and that was it. I did.

I just heard the Delaney and Bonnie album on Elektra and I just went through the roof. I nearly retired at that point. I figured there wasn't much point in playing anymore. I grant you that some of the songs may sound the same, but if they do, that is deceptive. I can't tell, because I never listen to my own recordings. Perhaps I should.

McGrath: So what's coming up with you in the near future?

Elton John: Well, there's going to be this bloody live album, and then there won't be anything from me for about six months. By that time we should have two albums ready. I just don't want there to be anything after the live album for a long time, because I think they are going to criticize the live album coming out, and they are going to get fed up with Elton John being rammed down their throats as I would be. I'm getting fed up with it.

McGrath: Is it being rammed down their throats so much in Britain as in North America?

Elton John: No, because there's only one radio station for a start, and so you don't get it rammed down your throat so much. The English people sort of reacted to me after I was a success in North America. The albums both went zooming up the charts and the new one came straight in at 20. They've been very nice to us. English audiences have been very understanding.

We (North America) have more criticism. Like the *Friends* album is going to be criticized more over here, but in England it's got rave reviews, so you win in both territories. I don't mind. You can't please everybody, for Christ sakes. I never intended to set out to please everybody. I can't believe it's all happened anyway. I don't believe we sold one million albums of *Elton John*—it seems ludicrous, cause at the time we made it, we were sort of knocked out when it came into the British charts at 47.

Life's very strange—it's really very strange. I don't think it's affected me as a person—I used to be equally outspoken—or the same sort of person I was before it happened. I've had so much hype and so many interviews that it's all really gotten over my head, and I've been able to handle it, because I'm sort of—if I'd have been 17 years old and just fresh out of college, I would probably been sort of—oh—I just don't want to think about it. So I—what does it all mean? I'm quite happy the way things are. I'm happy just to make music—and we left him sitting there, crying. (sic)

CROWBAR: WHATTA RUSH!

Bayshore Inn, Vancouver, August 15, 1971

THIS IS THE SECOND of two interviews with this quintessential Ontario bar band of the era. They made it big with *Oh, What A Feelin (Whatta Rush)* that marked the general optimism and youthfulness of the early Pierre & Maggie Trudeau years in Canadian politics.

Kelly Jay and the group lived west of Toronto, between Hamilton and Ancaster at a spread called "Bad Manors"—figures—and, in a sort of true Canadian fashion, Kelly was just as famous for his friends and acquaintances—Ronnie Hawkins and John Lennon—as he was for his musicianship. Heck, these guys could have backed Dylan!

It was a happy day when I heard Crowbar were playing in Vancouver. Just across from the *Georgia Straight* office, in fact, at *Gassy Jack's*. So I stomped on over, heard a set, re-established contacts with Kelly Jay, met the rest of the group and set up an interview for the next day, when fellow scribe Mike Quigley and I truck on down to their hotel and tape this monster first time out. The next two days I spent hanging out with the band, calling around and trying to organize a free concert at All Season's Park. Unfortunately, generators, trucks, and essential assistance seem to be lacking when I needed them, so nothing worked.

Rick McGrath: What's been happening since you played the Gardens?

Kelly Jay: Everything's happened, man. Amazing thing: we played Nanaimo. That was so much fun. That's where I want to go back to. I want to play Nanaimo again.

McGrath: Grease city.

Kelly Jay: I don't care, it was a great concert. All you could hear

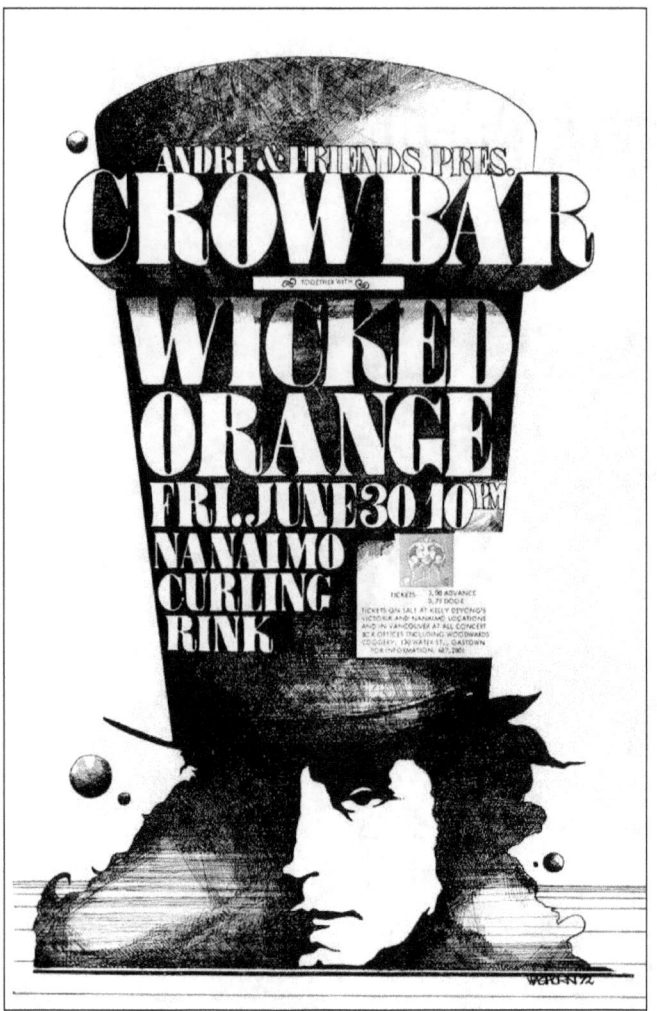

at the end of the show when the crowd left was the sound of meshing gears and rubber excruciating on the pavement. They got right into it so much. If there's anything I can't stand it's a cool audience. I've got my rights too, man, and I can't stand a cool audience. They just turn me right off. They just sit there and they're looking for things to cut up and they're not concentrating on the fact that there's somebody there serving their senses to try and alleviate some pressures or whatever. And they're there just to be critical or compare you to Alvin Lee or whatever. But Nanaimo was great—and The Gardens crowd was fine, too.

But we want to play all the areas around here, like Prince Rupert, Prince George, Victoria. I think what we should do is just move out here for six months and just play all over. After the Nanaimo show we went home to Ontario and recorded *Happy People* which was an experiment in terror. But it's what we wanted to do. We wanted to make a commercial record and we made a record that was palatable to people who don't particularly digest Crowbar. I think if that record had been released under some other band's name it would have been accepted. But we have some people say "That's not what Crowbar sounds like, it's totally non-indicative of the group, and consequentially I give it a one."

Mike Quigley: Out of what?

Kelly Jay: (laughs) Out of four million. It's got a good beat, easy to dance to...

McGrath: I give it an eight, Dick...

Kelly Jay: That's the thing. We did a record that we wanted. It's not the follow-up to *Oh, What A Feelin'* because it didn't have a follow-up and we've told everybody all along we're the smart-asses and big mouths and everything, that our records are not open to critical acclaim because they're things that we're creating on record. We don't know enough about recording yet to make masterpieces and I don't think people should say things against it until our fifth record. I don't think they should say that about anybody's record.

McGrath: Are you going to get into producing your own?

Kelly Jay: No, I don't think so, because when the group starts producing their own then they really start laying their own egos on the line and they start assassinating themselves. And that's like suicide. It's better to let somebody else make the decisions. First of all, though, you've got to watch your producer. It's got to be somebody who's got experience and does things that you like. One thing that we want to do is as many free concerts as people will set equipment up for us. It takes nothing for us to do a thing and it's more fun to do free things. The pressure is off and you can loosen up and it seems that you play better.

John Gibbard (guitar): It's the duty of every musician to get his rocks off every time he picks up his axe, because if he doesn't, he's being hypocritical.

Kelly Jay: The idea of having the great pleasure of seeing some international superstar sitting around in a coffee shop, idly playing with the local band and ripping off a few snazzy runs is a bunch of horseshit. Every time a musician picks up his guitar, like John sitting there rehearsing now (during the taping John was sitting on a bed practicing on his unamplified guitar) he should get it on. But I'm getting immune to it, like I don't even hear him. I can hum you every lick he's going to play, except for the new ones he's worked up. They're just as much a part of the group as the songs. They're not fillers. Like I really resent the American album which had them labelled as "Frenchman's Filler."

They're not, man, they're things that these guys sit down with those funny wooden things with those wires on it and that they can make those things do. Rheal Lanthier (guitar) has got a million of them. And they'll always be on our albums. Always.

McGrath: Tell us about your meeting with Pierre Trudeau.

Kelly Jay: OK. We got a letter just after we left here last time asking us if we would be interested working a job in Perth, Ontario. We sent them back a telegram saying forget it. Then we got another letter, this time a little more insistent, and they upped the money a little.

We knew it was for the City of Perth, and we knew it was for town festivities, we knew it was a free concert and the town was paying for it, right? So we figured—like at Scarborough High School you can accept a lower price because you know it's the students' council and they haven't got the bread—and you know you can go in and it'll be a good concert. But if it's for some town council that they'll write it off at the end anyway and call it highway tax or something. And the old coffers are just packed in those places. So we got some good bread out of it. So we sent back a letter saying, well, we don't know, and they sent back a note saying Pierre Trudeau was going to open the festival. We said, well, that's cool, and they said that would guarantee more money because we were working on a percentage of the gate and he was bound to draw 50 or 60 thousand. So we accepted the gig and all these mysterious things started happening.

We started getting phone calls from people asking us if there was any truth to the rumour that we knew Margaret Trudeau. There were rumours that Roly (Roly Greenway, bass) or me knew Margaret Trudeau in Vancouver before she was married. And we said, no, we didn't know her. But they kept insisting that she knew us. And we said, well, that's really neat man, groovy, she knows us.

Like, we know so many people. So then we get a phone call a week before the gig and the Secretary of State starts laying all this stuff on us like the Trudeaus would request—could we please reserve some time to talk to them and could we this and could we that, and we said, hey, we're travelling in heavy company.

So we said sure and they gave us a few things that said no guns, no explosives, please don't bring any narcotics or please this, that, and the other thing so we promised that we would be very straight and harmless and not carry any blunt objects or anything.

We showed up in Perth and they had done numerous security checks on us, like analyze our records to see if we were potential assassins.

Quigley: Like play them backwards.

Kelly Jay: Yeah, and hear Paul McCartney's phone number. Or his underwear size. So we arrive there and Trudeau arrives there in his big chopper with the exhaust pipes off, does two passes of the city and everybody knows that this big helicopter is going to land. And he's really got his presentation and thing together. So he lands and—you've got to picture the area that we played in— we played on a raft in the middle of a river. On a RAFT. We're getting shocks all night and it's raining, yeah.

John Gibbard: And this guy says don't go near the water because there might be a power line in it and there's enough voltage to kill a cow.

Kelly Jay: So, at any rate, they have this big stand set up behind us and then the pool, and then the area where the people sit and watch the band. When he arrives, Trudeau walks up on this ramp and they introduce him and they say things and when they're up on the thing we're all standing on the raft trying to figure out which one was him and there was this guy with a

Fair exchange
PM receives Crowbar pendant from Rolly Greenway

Party time in Perth: Prime Minister Pierre Trudeau cops a Crowbar pendant after the band's performance. Bottom photo: Trudeau and his wife, Margaret, at the concert.

fringe jacket and we thought it was Stomping Tom Connors or somebody and, shit, it turns out to be Pierre Trudeau.

And he just didn't look like he should.

So he came down the stairs and sat in his area to watch us. So we play and after the set we see Pierre and Sonnie (Sonnie Bernardi, drums) got a good line off. Trudeau asked us if we called ourselves Crowbar because we pried people's minds open, and Roly said, no, that Ronnie Hawkins gave us the name because we could mess up a crowbar in 10 seconds. And they all laughed and Sonnie said actually what Ronnie really meant is we could fuck up a crowbar in 10 seconds. And so we hung out with Trudeau and we gave him and Margaret one of our Crowbar necklaces—but Roly got it stuck over his head—actually his hair was so long on the back of his head that he got it stuck over his nose. And he was yanking it and it wouldn't move and so Roly pushed in his nose and pulled the chain over it.

And he said that *Oh, What A Feeling* was his favourite record. And he was interested in the music scene and all that, so we laid down this trip on him that we wanted to work in Canada. We worked LA, and it was groovy, but—just look out that window, those pine trees and mountains are just so much more impressive than palm trees. This fucking country is incredible. We want to stay in Canada. Nobody believes us when we say that.

McGrath: I believe you. Tell me a bit about it.

Kelly Jay: Crowbar is a group of six losers. We've been losers all along. When we played the bar circuits we were always too out of step, we didn't play enough top 40. We never got hired because our hair was too long and our tuxedos weren't pressed enough. When we did wear frilly shirts they were always too frilly and things like that.

John Gibbard: We went up to Timmons with these new Walking Suits and frilly shirts and everybody comes out and looks and yells "Fuckin' queers!"

Kelly Jay: No, really, they come after you with chain saws and things like that.

McGrath: A quick hair cut.

Kelly Jay: Yeah, cut your hair with a chain saw.

McGrath: If you had the opportunity of making the Canadian music scene any way you wanted it, what would you do?

Kelly Jay: First of all, I'd stop the total horseshit HYPE that just because a group is Canadian, it's good. You know what it's like?

It's like pushing a car to get it started...

McGrath: ...and finding out there's no gas in the tank?

Kelly Jay: Yeah. Like we've gone nuts with this CRTC thing. First Canadians had no talent and now all of a sudden Canadians are gods. We've been the garbage can of the United States; if a record didn't make it in California, they'd send it to Canada. They wouldn't send it to New York. That's why the whole story when we were a little dumber was that, as a country, we would say, "Wow, man, I went to Buffalo last weekend and picked up ten new Gene Vincent singles. They aren't even released up here, man, look at this, *Blue Jean Bop*. It won't be released for months and I'll be the rage at Maggie's party." And there was great exoduses going to Buffalo to pick up these singles. It was always a contest to see who could get Little Richard on the freakiest labels. It had to be black, yellow and cerise. And by doing all this to Canada, the guys in the States created a Frankenstein monster.

They created a culture of rock musicians that had just insane tastes. This band, Crowbar, we could sing *Take Good Care of My Baby* and make it sound great. That's because all the hip groovy people have forgotten that Bobby Vee did it first and they just remember it was a great song. But at the same time we could do things by Mose Allison or Ike and Tina Turner or James Brown, Otis Redding and all the heavy stuff, because we had a cross section of those records; I even used to buy Pat Boone records. I still play *Tennessee Saturday Night* and think it's one of the best boogie records ever made.

You know something? Mack Rebenack wrote a song on Frankie Ford's *Sea Cruise* album, which, by the way, was a monster album. But at that time Frankie Ford was really heavy into the rock and roll thing. Mack Rebenack wrote the songs. Mack Rebenack was also partners with Sonny Bono, of Sonny & Cher. Mack Rebenack is now Dr. John, the heaviest fuckin' dude in music today. And I love Dr. John, man, I really dig him. But he used to be Mack Rebenack, who wrote songs for Frankie Ford and played guitar on all those sessions. You know what I mean? It's such a fuckin' double standard. That's why we say to people, "Do you remember when your hair wasn't long or have you always been really neat?"

McGrath: Of course, you were really cool when your hair was short.

Kelly Jay: Of course you were. And if people didn't believe it, you'd kick the shit out of them.

McGrath: Now you just don't kick them.

Kelly Jay: Yeah, it's just peace, baby, and you try to get it together with his head.

John Gibbard: Groovy, baby, like outasight, man.

Kelly Jay: Nowadays, if somebody starts giving you static you just say let's sit down and rap about it. In the old days you'd back your '56 Ford over him.

McGrath: You'd start playing with the creases in your chinos and that would mean that your feet were ready.

Kelly Jay: I remember that. And I remember dances where guys would break Coke bottles and give it to you right in the face and think nothing of it. A good thing to do is carry an old photograph of yourself from about five or six years ago. Not a high school photograph, because that was horseshit too. That was the phoniest day of your life. And if you cut it all off today and dressed up like you did in 1966 people would instantly revert and treat you just like they would have then.

We just don't understand that their minds haven't progressed like ours. Their minds haven't been liberated. They haven't had time to smoke a joint and say, yeah, that park really is beautiful and those totem poles, think of how much work it took some cat to sit down and carve one of those. Where were those people's heads at that build all those totem poles?

McGrath: Not only that, they carved them out with jade chisels.

Kelly Jay: Jade?

McGrath: Yeah, I know this guy who collects Indian artefacts and he's got this piece that came from Stanley Park. It's deep green and honed down to a fine edge. No metal shit for those guys.

Kelly Jay: Yeah. We know this old guy in Brantford who collects Indian things and he's got this arrowhead made out of red quartz.

McGrath: Anyway, to get back to the hype thing we were talking about before.

Kelly Jay: Yeah, it's got to be changed. I believe in true advertising. Tasteful advertising. I hate garbage.

McGrath: That's different than hype, which infers that you're making something better than it really is. What else would you do?

Kelly Jay: The second thing, which is probably the most important thing, is the expression of oneself alone. Like each person in this band can do something entertaining on their own. Because the other five have given him the confidence. The other five have said that you're an entertaining person. You make me laugh or I like the way that you do this. So therefore it makes each person have some confidence in themselves and some conviction that they know they can do it.

Like Sonnie could be a stand up comedian. He's hilarious. He's a good actor. This band is being put together with a substantial background for movies. We're actually going to make an excellent movie some day. Not a *Help* movie or anything, but an extension of our music. Or our lives, which we like to attribute our music to. And most bands lack that. Most bands figure that you have to have this thing down that they need each other.

It's not true that you just go out and buy a Fender Telecaster and a super Bassman and just sit down and listen to Hendrix and Clapton and learn riffs and put them together. It's just not that. Any asshole can do that. If I see a band doing that I'm suddenly just turned off and I could care less. That's a pretty standard thing of people saying that you should like somebody else and the minute you say it you're dead. That's an old thing.

I honestly believe that if a kid is sixteen years old and he really wants to make it and he's embittered by the fact that he hasn't got a hit record, well, the kid should be taken aside by some older musician and taken into a dressing room somewhere and the older musician should get the kid stoned and then he should BEAT THE SHIT OUT OF HIM. He should break the kid's fuckin' arm and say now play. That's what it comes down to.

John Gibbard: Far out man, like outasite...

Kelly Jay: "Whiskey-a-Go-Go, eh, dad, that's really fucking cool and groovy and fuck you only play rock and roll" and I'd just like to lace one of these guys right in the mouth. Usually one of these guys has the talent of a clam. He plays as well as a clam. And you know a clam can do any lick that Eric Clapton can do. But they don't have anything to offer themselves. They don't say here's something I made up. Like Brahmin, I've heard nothing but rave reviews about them because they have a mime artist with the group. But I've never seen them.

One group I really liked from here for energy and for being a self-professed Top 40 band was the Night Train Review. They had a lot of energy and their horns were together. But there are some kids that come along. Like this Mark somebody I saw in New York.

Thirteen years old and I'd like to drop a piano on his head. Because he's really good. He just plays and shit does he sing. He's going to put an album out in the fall and when he does it's just goodbye Elton John. Elton John blew Feliciano off and this kid is going to get Elton John.

McGrath: I can't say I feel too badly because I really don't dig Elton John.

Kelly Jay: I think Elton was one of the grossest put-ons. Like, I can see that the cat plays excellent piano—and he's got some things but anyone who would put on a brand-new Porky Pig shirt with sparkly boots and then not wear them outside is just a little phoney.

John Gibbard: He's just a produced phenomena.

McGrath: He's like Paul Buckmaster's kid who's got stuck in his licks. And Buckmaster is getting a little thin too. Did you hear Leonard Cohen's new album? Well, Buckmaster arranged the strings and horns on it and guess what... right out of Elton John land.

Kelly Jay: Leonard Cohen, what a treat. That's like the first time I came here I found Don Franks living at the Ranch Motel, which is what he wanted to do, to be alone, and then talking to him because he was my hero all these years. Because he's so fucking grossly underrated. He had to be the stupidest man in show business because he always had these stupid parts in *Jericho*. One thing that always came through, though, was that he was the best in *Jericho*. He was always the most interesting character.

John Gibbard: Kelly, that show he did that opened and closed on Broadway in one day.

Kelly Jay: I've sat over in that hotel and listened to him sing boogie songs that I would pay five dollars to go and hear him sing. And even in *Finian's Rainbow* I could see that he wasn't happy being Woody. Sometime I'll do a whole thing on Don for you guys. We just can't let that man get away.

There's guys who really know. Directors and people. These transformers of entertainment. Without that your Lionel train doesn't go; the train is a gas but it needs the power that says when it goes. These assholes that are the transformers say now you can be good and no, no, now you're an eight millimeter home movie.

Those cats that do that know Franks is a genius. They know he won't do anything he doesn't want to do and now they're making him suffer. Well, me, and about five people like me are going to pull the plug on those motherfuckers, man.

Because the transformer is no good without the wall plug. And then there's going to be the fuse box, and then someone's going to say "Oh yeah, well I'm Niagara Falls," but sooner or later we'll get to them. But at least you can say to these people that are the moguls that they said: (to Franks) "I'm sorry, you badmouthed our star, Sheila Armpit, and she's much too valuable a property for you to fuck around. You're a nobody and you don't have appeal and we'll teach you that you can't do what you think you can do, artist smart-guy fascist pinko," and they start to get nasty.

McGrath: And a little confused, too.

Kelly Jay: Just check out these street musicians you've got here. Now that's a great thing. The most admirable people I've ever seen. They're out there getting their chops together and at the same time getting paid for it. And some of them are incredible musicians, really fine. And I would like to see that happen all across Canada. It would bring humanization back into music and it would reassert the fact that music is made by people and not by speakers with chrome covers on it.

Led Zeppelin: Fire In The Hole

Robert Plant at the Led Zeppelin Vancouver news conference. Photo by Stuart H. Clugston, courtesy Neptoon Records

The Pacific Coliseum, Vancouver, BC, August 19/20, 1971

AHHH, YES, LED ZEP... the seminal heavy metal band of the early 1970s. Let's face it, Robert Plant was The Frontman of the time, and Jimmy Page was by far The Axeman of his age. For me this was The Big Time, an exclusive interview with what was probably then the world's hottest—and heaviest—rock band.

Could it get any better?

Amazingly, yes—they let me watch the concert from the stage! For almost four hours I lurked about 20 feet away from Page, hidden from the audience by his massive mountain of speakers, watching him swirl and gyrate, his small, graceful hands wringing out musical magic as John Bonham beat the crap out of his drum kit, John Paul Jones fluctuated twixt bass and keyboards, and Plant whooped and wailed through the group's repertoire of the time—their first three albums. It was damned amazing. To make things even more interesting, as there was no Seattle gig on this tour about 4,000 Zepheads drove from the US to Vancouver for the show, only to discover there were no tickets available. They were not happy.

When I arrived early for the show I remember an army of Americans shouting, pounding and pushing on the glass entrance doors of the Pacific Coliseum. They kept it up until showtime when the promoters decided it was safer, and no doubt smarter, to simply let them in for free rather than risking the crowd crashing through the glass. As a result the Coliseum crowd swelled to about 20,000 fans, which meant the "festival seating" area in front of the stage was dangerously crammed with stoned zepheads. Yes, they did influence the concert.

Twice during the performance the band had to stop playing to let the roadies move their equipment back because the crush of fans was so thick they started to rip the front of the stage apart. Zany. Even with the interruptions it was one helluva show, culminating in *Dazed & Confused*, which at that time was their big final encore number.

After Zep's tumultuous concert all I had to do was wait for

the crowds to disperse and slip backstage: lots of cops, a few groupies (not surprisingly, more sophisticated than the usual fare) and the by-now-familiar faces that appeared backstage after every Big Concert. I found the usual sports team dressing rooms in the bowels of the building and waited for my cue.

After a half hour or so the door opened and band manager Peter Grant looked out and motioned me inside the dressing room. The boys looked like they were having fun, as well they might. Vancouver was the first date of a long North American tour, and spirits are helped considerably if the first night is a winner. I guess they figured 20,000 people trying to climb onstage was a good sign.

I made a beeline over to Page and Plant who were sitting off in a corner discussing, I thought, either a new song or part of an old one. Page was playing an acoustic guitar and singing, and Plant was listening intently.

In the middle of the room was a large table, covered with food and booze and general goodies. Wandering around it were Jones and Bonham, also flailing away on acoustic guitars and loudly singing old rock hits like *Save The Last Dance For Me* and *The Bristol Stomp*, stopping only to nosh on some food and drink.

Not exactly heavy metal. As the interview went on they got louder, and as soon as Page realized I wasn't going to ask him any guitar questions, he left Plant and I on our own and joined Jones & Bonham. It was quite infectious fun and on occasion during the interview Plant would become distracted and join in on some chorus. And then, of course, we hit midnight...

Rick McGrath: It was pretty hot out there...

Robert Plant: Yeah, sometimes it gets a bit scary when we see half the stage disappearing...

Jimmy Page: It was a bit rough.

McGrath: Has that happened before?

Jimmy Page: No, never. I was wondering if there was going to be any stage left by the time we finished.

McGrath: It seemed to me you tried to control them, musically.

Jimmy Page: It didn't work.

Robert Plant: Usually people just throw stuff at us—it was bloody shocking to lose the front of the stage. I didn't think you could tear them apart.

Jimmy Page: It seems you can.

McGrath: Yeah, it was damned amazing, and we're all still alive. OK. Let's talk about what you've been doing since you were here last year. Tours. Records.

Jimmy Page at the Led Zeppelin Vancouver news conference.   Photo by Stuart H. Clugston, courtesy Neptoon Records

Robert Plant: We've been to Italy, Switzerland, Denmark. We did a tour of England, intending to go back to all the old clubs that we played in the beginning.

McGrath: Around Birmingham?

Robert Plant: All those sorts of places. In some way it was a successful move, in other ways it was a bit of a dead loss, because you'd be playing in places that only hold 250 people.

McGrath: Isn't that what the club trip is like in England? A lot of smaller, intimate halls?

Robert Plant: Yeah, that's what it used to be like at the beginning. But there's always something bigger than a club in each town, a hall or something. Not so much a Coliseum, though.

McGrath: Denmark? Isn't that where you played together first?

Jimmy Page: Yes, as the New Yardbirds. It was fun going back.

Robert Plant: This time we actually made some money.

McGrath: Sounds cool, but didn't you have some problems in Milan?

Robert Plant: We went to Milan, and there was a big music festival with people from all countries contributing. They travel around, and we just came for one gig. And we were told that it was a cool thing and even though there was a reputation for bottles being thrown in Rome, we were assured it wouldn't happen to us. Anyway, we started playing in a big cycle arena, and they'd been booing everybody else, and as soon as we walked onstage, I noticed some smoke at the back of the arena. And there's all this smoke and there's firemen behind us and I was going Fire! Fire! in my finest Italian.

Anyway, nobody took any notice of me and we carried on for about a quarter of an hour and the fire had gotten all around us. And I turned around and looked at everybody and then I saw Peter Grant—his eyes had all gone big and red. And everybody was suddenly coughing. People suddenly appeared with masks and things like that and suddenly there were bombs going off, everywhere. And the whole thing about what I'm doing is that I've been doing it seven years and I'm—what time is it?

McGrath: Midnight.

Robert Plant: I am now 23.

McGrath: Your birthday? Well, let me be the first to congratulate you (we shake hands and behind us Jimmy, John Bonham and John Paul Jones break into a heavy metal acoustic version of Happy Birthday to You. By this time I'm starting to eye the table of food and wondering if Robert has forgotten about the Milan fire. He hadn't.)

John Paul Jones at the Led Zeppelin Vancouver news conference. Photo by Stuart H. Clugston, courtesy Neptoon Records

Robert Plant: And so it's been seven years onstage and suddenly I find we've been tear gassed. So I got an Italian guy to come on and I told him to tell everybody to (Robert purses his lips and blows several times). And everybody's blowing. And everyone was just sitting down and coming around and digging it. And I was getting so I couldn't sing, and the feeling, if you've ever been tear-gassed, is that if you move, you've got 15,000 kids who are going to freak out. So you don't move and you become so nauseated. Anyway, it finally broke up and there were kids running everywhere.

I forgot to tell you, as we arrived, there were wagons all alongside the road, and there were 250 storm-troopers standing in line up by the front door. So I jumped out of the car and I was saluting and shouting and checking the uniforms and walking up and down the ranks going (makes faces) and I saw something I've never seen before, because they were completely devoid of anything human. They just looked at me as if to say Objective Number One or something.

But back to the fire and concert. Suddenly everyone was running. When the kids started running over the stage we split and ran down a passage under the cycle arena. And then they tear-gassed the passage. So Peter, who can't run very fast, was in trouble. So we found a room and we barricaded ourselves in. We broke into a medical cupboard and had all these fucking weapons and stuff. It was crazy. We opened the door and they were bringing the roadies in unconscious. We had one nurse and some oxygen and we looked out the window into the streets and there was fighting and shooting and cars being smashed and driven into trees and the whole thing was like a war. And it was because we stood up on stage?

But that was not the real reason for it all. There were 250 storm troopers who just didn't know what the fuck was going on. Fifteen thousand people are jumping in the air trying to escape the fucking tear gas and they don't understand. And as we drove back to the fucking hotel, round the wrecked cars and round the fights and all that, there were roadside hospitals all the way to the center of Milan. I've never seen anything like that.

I got up the next morning and got the papers and the driver translated and just told us that the kids had caused a riot and the police had to move in and do the fucking honours. People lost their sight. I cried for days and days and every time I think about it—or I think of something gentle, I even saw a silly film with Cary Grant in it, and he was going on about what man must do to be man—I was fucking crying. Because it just fucking hit me and if I'm ever down in America all somebody has to do is say, "Are you a boy or a girl?" and I'll fucking dive at him. Because it's an animal reaction. I've already been in a rathole once. And I know it's not just because we're radicals or rock'n'rollers. It's because there's nobody understanding. Our side of the fence is going over there and saying *Fuck That*, and their side is coming over and saying *Up Yours*, and it's the wrong thing, you know. The concerts should be in twice as big a place and everybody should bring their parents. And then we can get it together. What we need is more of a bridge between the two sides... and in Milan? What are you going to do?

McGrath: Well, you've finished your new album.

Robert Plant: Haha yes. We finished that, and we did it in our own home. Well, how it went was that we used a mobile truck

for our recording unit and we went to an old manor in Surrey. There we put up all the equipment in one room and stuck all the mike leads through a window. Straight into the recording van. So anything that we did just went straight down on tape. Bit by bit it grew up into a great collage of numbers.

McGrath: Do you like it?

Robert Plant: (nodding head) Yeah. It was another atmosphere altogether.

Jimmy Page: We needed a break from the intense touring we had gone through with the first two albums. After working almost 24 hours a day we managed to back off and take off for a couple of months rather than a couple of weeks. We went off and rented a cottage with no electricity—a contrast to touring hotel rooms. Obviously, it had quite an effect on the album.

McGrath: What are your thoughts on Led Zeppelin III?

Robert Plant: I am really happy with it, because to me it was just one step in growing up.

McGrath: Well, it got some bad press. That's something we should talk about later. But there was an incredible wave of Led Zeppelin mania, or whatever, and you had just finished a very successful tour, and then the album came out and nothing happened.

Robert Plant: Yeah, but to me, personally, that album was certainly a large step after the second one. Because you can't keep turning out the same thing. If you do that, you can't do anything for yourself. We know we can rely on things like *Whole Lotta Love* and it is quite easy to work within the same framework all the time. But who does that? Just people who haven't got anything going for them in the brains, that's who. And I think the third album was an essential thing, I don't care if it sold any copies at all, because it showed there was a bit more attached to us and it than *Shake Your Money-Maker* sort of stuff.

Jimmy Page: The influence of living in the cottage gives the album a pastoral, acoustic feeling. It has that feeling because that's how it was. After all the deep intensity of touring for years it was just a totally opposite feeling. There's an emotional quality in my songs and sharing that feeling is what I think music is about.

McGrath: Which leaves you in the bind of wanting to progress, when the audience doesn't want you to.

Robert Plant: I daren't say they don't want you to, but it seems they're not ready to accept, or even give it a fair try, because I think if people play the third album and listen to it with the same amount of justification that they gave the second one, they might see what's going on.

McGrath: What about rock critics? They seem to be the other extreme. On one hand you have the audience screaming Whole Lotta Love, and on the other a critic saying the opposite.

Robert Plant: Well, a critic who's been a critic in one position for more than six months gets a bit cocky, right? He feels pretty cool. So he suddenly starts making assumptions and statements that aren't his to make, man. You can't condemn something just by—a critic can't fucking state what he wants to—like if he goes to a concert, like tonight, and he goes away and writes, "Well, I don't know what to say because it wasn't too good at all." For 20,000 people going it was fucking too much, but that one guy could get quite a reputation for decrying it. And unfortunately that seems to be the general system of critics—to make themselves a name. Instead of just transposing what happens, and saying it was accepted, they suddenly start becoming an entity for themselves, instead of a courier for the people.

And just as a new society is growing and moving, we've got to eliminate all this old crap and we've got to be fair with each other. Because if we get all these blasé attitudes at an early stage where we're still trying to prove to a lot of people that it's a wholesome, positive thing and they keep tearing away inside it, well, it'll be ruined before it's even gotten halfway. Because that attitude doesn't stop just at music, but it goes everywhere.

And that attitude of somebody in a position to influence somebody else is open to somebody with no talent but a pen and a job. And it worries me, really, because I don't just see it for us, I see it for people who I really fucking admire. They've given something and are working really hard. And people are digging it and going out and getting some satisfaction from it. But that guy, well, he's on another one altogether, isn't he?

McGrath: Right, I think a critic is no good unless he has constructive or positive things to say. That's part of criticism. It should help more than hinder.

Robert Plant: Yes, but things like *Rolling Stone* magazine get out of hand. Even in England people buy it because it's been around for such a long time. It gets to be a habit. And what they read is something else, man. Because it's always down, down, down. Why don't they stop all that and start being nice? Is that such a hard thing to do?

McGrath: Yeah, but they're in it for the bucks and controversy always sells more than good news.

Robert Plant: Yeah, but we're in it for a buck as well, to an extent. But we go out there and there's no bad ones. People could throw a fucking bottle and it would still be cool because they're there and the thing incites them to do that. So you just ride along with it.

McGrath: They ripped the doors off the front of this place tonight.

Robert Plant: They've been eating good breakfast cereals or else they've captured energy in long hair.

I wonder if any of them were in your Gastown riot. We heard about it, but see, when you're in our position, mate, you're in so many fucking places in such a short time and everybody's going look at this, and people keep coming up and saying what do you think about them saying this and what do you think about them saying that? Half the time you miss it or you just don't even know it's there. Because if you get affected by these things, well, you just go on stage shivering, more or less.

McGrath: I've noticed the stage act has changed since you were here last. It seems to be getting back to a hard rock and blues thing.

Robert Plant: Well, it ain't wanting to change, it's just how it goes. Tomorrow is another day. It's like with albums. People say "Do you follow in the same pattern as before?" And you talking about the third album. The third album, to me, was a disappointment in the way it was accepted because it wasn't given enough of a chance. After *Heartbreaker* and *Bring It On Home*. And thunder, which was what it was.

So we say, "Try this for size" and I thought when we were doing it I was able to get inside myself a little more and give a little more on the album. I thought the whole thing felt like that. I was pleased with it, and I'd play it now without hesitation and dig it. And you can't always do that to an album that you've played a million times. But I really thought it stood up and then everybody was saying, well, noo, and they'd leave it and then come back in a couple of weeks time and say, well, we can see—but, nevertheless, we think it's best.

But that's what people say because the simple, heavy thunder is much easier to assimilate, much easier to react to in every way. But you can't just do that, otherwise you become stagnant and you're not really doing anything, you're just pleasing everybody else. The whole thing about the whole music scene now is that we didn't follow Sam the Sham, we didn't follow all those people.

We came over here and nobody knew who we were and we weren't following anything. We weren't saying, "It's Gary Puckett for us, and come over here"—do you know what I mean? And it's just by playing what we had to do, with all the bollocks that we got, that people said fair enough. And anything we can do new on an album I think is a good move.

McGrath: What direction is your new material taking?

Robert Plant: It really varies, Because having that place in the country—it's that old cliché about a place in the country—but it was really great. The mikes coming in through the windows and a fire going in the hearth and people coming in with cups of tea and cakes and people tripping over leads, and the whole thing is utter chaos.

Bonzo's drums are in the hall, in the entrance hall, with one mike hanging from the ceiling. And things like that. And everyone's going—and we set up anther set of drums and I was playing drums—and it was a good feeling, and we did it as easy as pie. So this album's got a lot of feeling to it.

Don Van Vliet: I'm a Soft Star.

Pacific Coliseum, Vancouver, September 17, 1971

IT WAS EASIER to get to talk with Don Van Vliet, *a.k.a.* Captain Beefheart, than one might have first imagined. Such is the narrowcast fame of the cult artist. After arriving at the back doors of the Pacific Coliseum around eight-thirty and jedi-like talking my way past the ever-vigilant security guards, it was rather surprising to almost walk into him, standing outside his dressing room, wearing a natty little black suit, holding a clarinet case, and showing off his finely manicured goatee. All under his stylish fedora. With his wife!

In my often-haphazard style of work I admit nothing had been set up in advance to prepare The Captain for any interviews, so I just introduced myself, flashed the microphone, indicated I was friendly, and he consented to talk. A suggestion we go somewhere to sit was declined, as he had been sitting a lot, and he liked to be standing.

This was fine with me, but it resulted in a few quirky moments later when some over-zealous and quite drunk fans started yelling about Frank Zappa (a touchy subject with The Captain) and generally making idiots of themselves. And then the crazy cats from the local radio stations—well, read on...

Rick McGrath: What can you say about your new album?

Don Van Vliet: The name of it is *Lick My Decals Off*...

Don's Wife, Janet: No, it isn't...

Don Van Vliet: Well, which one do you mean?

McGrath: The one you just mentioned...

Don Van Vliet: It's called *The Spotlight Kid*.

McGrath: No more decals?

Don Van Vliet: You say "deck-alls" up here.

McGrath: And you say "dee-calls" down there... it's a bit different.

Don Van Vliet: It slows it down a bit, but that doesn't matter. The words slow it down more than that.

McGrath: Is there any point in asking for a musical description of the new album? Is that possible, anyway?

Don Van Vliet: No, I don't think there is any way to describe it. It's a little more accessible, I think. A lot more accessible.

McGrath: Can we talk about your earlier albums? The first was Captain Beefheart and The Magic Band. And then the next one we hear about is the Blue Thumb one. And there's a whole bunch that have been released in between. Why have these come out just recently?

Don Van Vliet: *Mirror Man* was released eight months ago, and I didn't even know it was coming out.

McGrath: Where was that recorded?

Don Van Vliet: That was recorded in a studio when I was with Kama Sutra.

McGrath: How many albums did you cut with them?

Don Van Vliet: There's more.

McGrath: There's still more they haven't released?

Don Van Vliet: Yeah.

McGrath: Are they releasing them with your name all over them?

Don Van Vliet: Well, they didn't give me any money. And they never have.

McGrath: Is there any chance of you starting up your own operation?

Don Van Vliet: Sure.

Fan: Maybe you could ask him when he's going to work with Zappa again.

Don Van Vliet: I'm not. No, I shouldn't have even worked with him when I did. Because I can't work. He works, I play. There's a difference. Are you talking about *Willie The Pimp*?

Fan: Yeah. Is that the only thing you've done with him?

Don Van Vliet: Yeah.

McGrath: You didn't like it?

Don Van Vliet: I didn't mind doing it, but he turned my voice down so far it was almost corny. I really sang that thing. And it turned it way down. He didn't tell me it was going to be turned down like that, and when he put it on I thought it was humourous. He should have gotten Johnny Rivers.

Fan: Well, that's how he is, I guess.

Don Van Vliet: How is he?

Fan: Pretty weird.

McGrath: You may not like it, but you could say Frank knows what he's doing.

Don Van Vliet: Well, I think people who know what they're doing to that degree aren't doing very much.

McGrath: Yeah, I think I know what you mean.

Don Van Vliet: That's what I mean.

McGrath: Could you tell me a bit more about this "play" concept you have of music.

Don Van Vliet: Music is play. For instance, a child playing in a yard, right? A child playing in a yard doesn't like to be called by his mother. I imagine the child wouldn't even quit playing if it weren't for someone disturbing him. So that's what I mean.

Some Radio Newsguy: Is this your first trip to Canada?

Don Van Vliet: Yeah, it's beautiful.

Some Radio Newsguy: Did you fly up?

Don Van Vliet: Yeah, it's beautiful.

Radio News Interviewer: Thanks.

Fan: Have you been to the east at all?

Don Van Vliet: No, but I'd like to go.

One Fan To Another: This guy said Zappa was a jerk for letting him do it to him...

Don Van Vliet: If God's doing the Jerk, is it the Jerk's fault for letting him do it to him?

McGrath: Pretty funky. You should hire these guys to come out and warm up the audience for you...

Don Van Vliet: They are the audience.

Some Radio Newsguy: Is there any chance you and Frank will kiss and make up?

Don Van Vliet: No.

Some Radio Newsguy: There isn't, eh?

McGrath: Well, you guys aren't at odds with each other, are you?

Don Van Vliet: No no no no no.

McGrath: You went to school together, didn't you?

Don Van Vliet: No, I never went to school. But it's not that I'm at odds with Frank. It's just that I don't wish to be around him. I'm interested in playing, not working.

McGrath: Do you still play at sculpting?

Don Van Vliet: Oh yeah. Painting, writing—and I've got a movie that's coming out soon.

Fan: Did you ever have the impression that you got known by being on Zappa's album?

Don Van Vliet: I don't think so.

Fan: That's how I knew you.

Don Van Vliet: Is that how you know me? Well, then I don't think you know who I am if you consider me in the same category as Frank Zappa.

Fan: That's not what I was saying.

(At this point the two fans are spotted by two of their friends. A yelling contest ensues)

Don Van Vliet: I don't want to talk about Frank Zappa. Let Frank Zappa speak for Frank Zappa, and I'll speak for Captain Beefheart.

Some Radio Newsguy: Tell me, are the guys in your group right now the ones who started with you, or are they changing all the time?

Don Van Vliet: No, I don't change all the time. The drummer is the one that started out with me. The other fellows have been with me about three years. The way the group is now has been happening for about two years.

Fan: Have you got a cigarette?

Don Van Vliet: Do you want a cigarette? (gives him one).

McGrath: Is your cousin still playing with the band?

Don Van Vliet: No, he's still in the red wings, fixing his eyes.

McGrath: I hope this tapes.

Some Radio Newsguy: Have you got any questions to ask?

Don Van Vliet: (pauses) Uh, yeah... are you doing a good job of not having any smog here?

Fan: Is the war in Viet Nam a vertical conundrum?
Some Radio Newsguy: Yeah, I think we're keeping it down. We have a bit of smog, but it's getting better (people start yelling).

Another Radio Newsguy: Have you ever met Wild Man Fisher?

Don Van Vliet: No, but I've seen him.

Another Radio Newsguy: Is he really insane?

Don Van Vliet: I believe in varying degrees of disconnection. I don't believe in insanity.

Another Radio Newsguy: Do you believe he's disconnected?

Don Van Vliet: No. He got away from Frank Zappa and Herbie Cohen, so I guess he isn't that disconnected.

Some Radio Newsguy: When are you going to discover Frank Zappa?

Don Van Vliet: Discover him?

Some Radio Newsguy: Yeah. Debut him on one of your albums.

Don Van Vliet: I don't even think about him, really. Most people say something about him.

McGrath: You've said you don't believe in drugs. Is there any reason for that?

Don Van Vliet: I think people should give themselves more credit. I think they have everything themselves. I don't think anything needs to be induced. Do you know what I mean?

McGrath: Yeah.

Don Van Vliet: I think they just get disconnected.

McGrath: Can you offer any suggestions why so many people do drugs?

Don Van Vliet: Because they want to, I guess. What I'm saying is that I just don't take them. Nobody in the group takes them.
Another Radio Newsguy: This is the first time you've been to Canada?

Don Van Vliet: Yeah.

Another Radio Newsguy: Is there a tour starting? Are you going around to other places?

Don Van Vliet: Yeah. We were on a tour of the States about six months ago.

Another Radio Newsguy: Are you going anywhere after here?

Don Van Vliet: This is my wife, Janet.

Janet: Hi.

Don Van Vliet: It's getting a bit claustrophobic. (We are surrounded by people)

Another Radio Newsguy: What's it like being the wife of a pop star?

Janet Van Vliet: It's nice.

Another Radio Newsguy: It is, eh?

McGrath: The Captain's not a pop star.. he's a rock star

Don Van Vliet: I'm not a rock star. I'm a soft person. I'm not a rock.

McGrath: That's interesting... a soft star.

Don Van Vliet: What?

McGrath: Soft star.

Another Radio Newsguy: How come you haven't been here before?

Don Van Vliet: Well, I never had enough money to make it up here. I never had enough money to get any equipment until recently. Believe it or not.

Another Radio Newsguy: Do you dig it?

Don Van Vliet: Do I dig it? Of course I do.

Fan: Where's Larry Fisher?

Don Van Vliet: I don't know. Your guess is as good as mine. You see, Zappa tried to connect me to a group of people in order to hold me back.

Fan: Awww.

Second Fan: Did he fuck you?

Don Van Vliet: Out of money? Most certainly.

Fans: Woo-woo. (and assorted screams)

Third Fan: Yes. I talked to a guy who knew Don Ellis and he said the same thing.

Don Van Vliet: Well, I sure didn't get any money. Ask Artie, he'll tell you. Artie!

Fan: Yeah, the percussionist. He played with Zappa for a long time.

Another Radio Newsguy: I'm not really interested in Zappa right now.

Don Van Vliet: Yeah. But you should be interested in Ed Marimba.

Art Tripp: Yeass?

McGrath: As chief percussionist for the Magic Band, Mr Marimba, perhaps you could tell me something about your background. Where did you do your regular drumming before?

Art Tripp: I've never done regular drumming. No, I've never got too serious about playing the drums. I've never got too serious about anything.

McGrath: What about the weird rhythm things you get into?

Art Tripp: I don't know—it's just something everybody can understand. It's not meant to be anything one way or the other. You hear it all every time you hear a train.

McGrath: Could you tell me a bit about your experiences with Zappa?

Art Tripp: Horrible.

McGrath: In what way did he give you a bad time?

Art Tripp: He really didn't want anyone to play. I had a good time for about five or six months, and then I found out he was stealing all my ideas, and I didn't want any of the fucking credit. I just wanted to do them. And then he was extremely hard to talk to. I'd try to start a conversation with him, and he'd just give me a lot of jive, huckster shit. He stole about 80% of his stuff from Don.

(At this point the Radio Newsguy and Beefheart are talking about cars. Radio news has a Willy Jeep and he's "dickering" for a 1914 something. Grease city.)

McGrath: Your music is pretty heavy for some people.

Don Van Vliet: I don't mean it to be...

McGrath: Obviously, because you keep on playing it.

Don Van Vliet: I'm not doing it for spite or anything—I just think it's nice to hear something different. I think they need something different. Maybe if they hear me and think my music's far out and they find out we don't do drugs then they won't take drugs either.

McGrath: Then they can do it themselves?

Don Van Vliet: Right. That's what I do. That's what all of us do. I would rather look at a rose than take drugs. When I want to look at a rose, I want to look at a rose.

McGrath: What do you think of the traditional performer/audience trip?

Don Van Vliet: I'd like to get them together as one, but every time the audience tries to do that, the police get a chance to beat people. And I don't like that. So I think it should be kept to a stage, performer and audience. It's probably better that way because I don't like to see kids get hurt.

McGrath: What's happening in the states these days?

Don Van Vliet: It's horrible, man. I just wrote a song that says, "Today's the day that everybody gets an oil well whether they like it or not."

Yet Another Radio Newsguy: Come the revolution, is that it?

Don Van Vliet: Pardon me?

Some Radio Newsguy: Come the revolution?

Don Van Vliet: (dazed) I don't know about the revolution. I don't think blood will cure oil. I think blood should be in a human body, and I think oil should be underground, and I think the rivers and oceans should be rivers and oceans. I have a painting that I did with a porpoise running into a watermelon at 800 miles an hour. And that was an apology statement.

Yet Another Radio Newsguy: A porpoise running into a watermelon?

Don Van Vliet: Yeah, crashing into one.

Yet Another Radio Newsguy: Are you a racist?

Don Van Vliet: No, no... don't you understand? The thing had to jump out of the ocean because it was getting burned up.

McGrath: But doesn't it seem realistic to think that any kind of ecological action depends on the upheaval of the current system?

Don Van Vliet: Well, I don't think another war will help. I think that people should write in about it. That they should sit down and write everybody a letter. To see if that works, you see? There's no doubt about it, most people are sitting on their ass, smoking a joint. Why aren't they doing something about it? Aren't they intelligent? Don't they listen? I've been saying these things in my music for the past seven years and nobody's been listening. I'm not intimidated, though.

Yet Another Radio Newsguy: I think people are listening to your music.

Don Van Vliet: Very few. Either that or the record companies aren't getting the music to the people. Which is probably what it is. I prefer to believe that.

McGrath: Could we talk a bit about your poetry. Is it spontaneous, natural verse, like your music, or do you work it out?

Don Van Vliet: I never plot. I leave that to the ad men who do the ads for Forest Lawn. I don't read the classics. I've never read a book.

McGrath: Never read a book?

Yet Another Radio Newsguy: I've read three in my life.

Don Van Vliet: When English is used for pleasure I think that's fine, but when it's used to tell people to make their eyes as small as the person who wrote the book, then I don't like it.

McGrath: Yeah, but you could also make people's eyes as big as the author's.

Don Van Vliet: But that would be very bad, man, because you see it's not good to look through other people's eyes. I find a "c" very bad because it isn't total. At this point I'm going to tickle you.

I'm just thinking about what you're saying.

Don Van Vliet: Don't think about what I say. It's all right. It depends on who's writing the English. If they're nice people, that's good. If they're bad that's no good.

McGrath: It's human communication.

Don Van Vliet: You know what I'm trying to do with the English language, don't you. I bet you know that.

McGrath: I know what you're doing. It doesn't matter what the words are, it matters what the sounds are in the words. Deck-all. Dee-cal.

Don Van Vliet: That's right. (laughs)

Red Robinson: Vancouver's DJ

Radio CKLG Studios, Vancouver, January, 1972

I DIDN'T GROW UP in Vancouver, so the first time I ever saw Red Robinson live and in in person was at The Beatles concert in Vancouver's Empire Stadium on August 22, 1964. He was the emcee who stopped the lads mid-show to clear away some of the piled-up bodies of overwhelmed girls from the feet of the Fab Four, eliciting John Lennon's famous command to "Get the fuck off our stage."

John didn't grow up in Vancouver, either, so he wouldn't have known, even in 1964, Red was already famous as one of Canada's first rock'n'roll radio and concert impresarios. He was *Vancouver's DeeJay*.

By 1972 Red had given up on the deejay game and was working in sales (he had The Voice) for CKLG, one of Vancouver's top pop music stations. Fellow scribbler Mike Quigley and I talked with him in one long session at 'LG, and walked away with a surprisingly detailed overview of early rock radio, performers, the players and the action during this unique period of musical history. And why not? Hey, this was a guy who had rubbed shoulders with all the very early rock'n'rollers, who had hung with Elvis and Buddy Holly, and who had basically provided the soundtrack to Vancouver's first youth culture. In 1994 Red was elected to the Rock and Roll Hall of Fame in Cleveland, Ohio, as a pioneer disc jockey, one of only three from Canada, and of 90 deejays overall. This interview was the first Mike and I did for *The Grape*.

Rick McGrath: Red, how did rock 'n' roll start out in Vancouver?

Red Robinson: All right. Here's what happened: I'm going to King Ed (King Edward—a local high school), and radio in Vancouver at that time was ending an era of soap operas, syndicated transcripts, and network. The Canadian Broadcasting Corporation was very strong with two networks going at the time: the Dominion network of the CBC and the Canada network. Most private stations featured so many hours of this programming. They had to—it was the law—because the CBC was the law. We didn't have an independent body—they were our bosses.

So, anyway, as these shows were dying I was at CJOR as a kid, just 16, just bumming around because it fascinated me. You know, the fact that you could communicate ideas—I was on my way to a commercial art thing—and radio fascinated me.

I thought, I love this kind of music, so what happened was this: a guy had a show on afternoons on CJOR, Hal Jordan, and in 1954 he's one of the best commercial announcers in the city.

It was sort of a half-hour teen thing. In those days everything was labelled teen. But you have to relate to the era. There was no such thing as a youth culture then because that culture grew with the music. A teenager was between 12 and 20. You were a kid, an adult, or in this funny little nothing middle group called teenager.

But as we talk through this thing, don't ever forget the significance of the youth culture growing and the youth attitude growing in conjunction with music. That is the really interesting part of it all.

So, getting back to this half-hour show that Hal Jordan hosted. It was his own and it was the only thing you listened to because it was aimed at you if you were in that age group. But this half-hour show was really going nowhere. Jordan quit, and went to Hamilton, Ontario.

They gave me the half-hour show and I started inserting Wyonie Harris and some of the things that you feel are happening with your age group. And the show grew. It grew from 30 minutes to an hour to two hours, and these were the days when a disc jockey show being two hours was (gives a long whistle).

There was only one real disc jockey in town—Jack Cullen—who is now sort of a legend. But the fact is that he was the only jock that anybody really knew. But I never listened to Canadian radio. I listened to American radio. And there were things happening. There was a guy on the west coast in Los Angeles called Al Jarvis, who was one of the first people to get into this kind of music. You could actually hear him at night, because the dial wasn't crowded. Then, about late 1954, a guy called Bob Salter went into Seattle on KJR and started doing the same thing. And I was doing it in Vancouver. Remember, in the west we think north and south, not east west. I started injecting more music and the show grew and no one knew what was going on. The next thing I know, while still going to King Ed school, within a year I had two and a half hours in the afternoon, 3:30 to 6:00, then 9:00 to 9:30 at night, and then a break for another Dominion network show, and then 10:00 to 1:00 in the morning. OK, so why would a station allow that? Because as these old shows were leaving, and as the old salesmen couldn't see what to sell, all of a sudden there was this market opening up.

And in radio, they found that advertisers were interested in selling merchandise to the youth market. But it was a fight to even say that they had any money. They used to say, "what do they buy, bubble gum and pop?"

Mike Quigley: What was the audience reaction to your show?

Red Robinson: Unbelievable. The adult reaction was that some kind of a bad thing was happening. Really bad. And I was polluting the airwaves. I faced nothing but abuse, but I think anybody who is pioneering anything does. And some of my old scraps show columns which say riots at Vincent Massey High in New Westminster. I had gone there to do a noon hour thing, playing records, mind you—no bands.

McGrath: Were they record hops?

Red Robinson: No, just a concert at lunch time. I'd play records and talk about the music—what it means, what they're trying to say. And the kids would clap their hands to the music and they called it a riot. It's funny now, but I faced all that abuse for years. Everybody putting it down, and the newspapers looking to grab you—"what is this? What is this guy doing and what is this music all about?" I was sort of the pied piper leading the innocents over the wharf. Because anything new I think people are frightened of. They don't understand it. So after the show became popular, this showed there were a lot of kids in town who were really picking up on this new music, this rock'n'roll. Obviously, the kids who were musically inclined were going to start picking up on it.

Then the groups started. Well, I've got to back up. Because of one thing—as Ray Charles told me in a great interview—the guy who made it all possible was Elvis Presley. Forgetting everything else you might think about him, because what he did—if you read Jerry Hopkins' book—he made it so interesting and fascinating to do the black thing. And he also faced all the abuse, you gotta go back and read—they said he was a pervert—it was unreal to watch.

Elvis took compositions from people like Clyde Otis and Otis Blackwell and he made them popular. He had a natural way of presenting the black man's music so you couldn't originally tell if it was Clyde McPhatter or Elvis Presley when he sang. When you found out later that Elvis was white instead of black, then you were really zapped. Because you didn't believe it—you thought he was black. And this was his claim to fame.

We were all influenced by the black man's music—it said something to you that nothing else had previously. For my generation, right? So he was the catalyst that made it happen. Because he became so big so fast and had so much influence it was now possible for others to come on and perform. He made it possible for the whole black world, as Ray Charles said, to be exposed to the white world. A whole generation. And there is a parallel here, because while Elvis was happening, so was rock radio, with guys like Alan Freed, Hound Dog Lorenz in Buffalo, and every little market. Of course, as the record thing grew, the jocks in each market were exposing more of it, and it became a thing, right? It swept the country in about three years.

McGrath: And then it hit the movies.

Red Robinson: It saved movies just like it saved radio. Without this music, radio was groping. The disc jockey was a new thing. The media opened up. It had to combat television and it simply became a matter of economics.

Quigley: How long were you at CJOR?

Red Robinson: I started there in 1954 part time and I stayed until March of 1957. Success is a funny thing. One reason I left CJOR is that for two and a half years I had 52% of the Vancouver radio audience when I was on the air. Because at that point everybody wanted to be a part of what was happening. It was so new.

Quigley: It was like an epidemic of sorts.

Red Robinson: It was like an epidemic because it was so much fun. And it provided a dance form, too. You have to remember that. Then it mattered. A new, exclusive generation dance that was not Glen Miller's. It was something their own.

McGrath: How did you format your radio show?

Red Robinson: Free form, basically, as you should in good FM today. You felt the mood of your show as you went along and you planned accordingly. You didn't really start tabulating sales and things like that until later on. You just felt it and then played it. And as people responded and you had more and more records, then you had to put some forms on it.

McGrath: What was the first group that you remember? That were actually playing rock 'n' roll.

Red Robinson: Well, it was always the black groups. And for every one of them you had a counter white group. You had the Penguins, and their white counterparts were the Crewcuts. And you had—well, there were so many—The Orioles.

McGrath: What about Vancouver groups?

Red Robinson: Right. We had a talent search—it was an idea of mine—in 1955 and, of course, part of the talent search was to find somebody who could sing like Elvis Presley. This was going on all across North America. Out of that talent search we found a band of different types of musicians who styled themselves after Bill Haley. So we took the lead singer, who was a Presley type, and put him with the Haley-type band.

I was the first guy in this province, and in fact Washington state or anywhere, to start taking the band and the music on the road. I'd go to Nanaimo and Prince Rupert and all the little towns up and down Vancouver Island, the Fraser Valley and the interior and I'd expose all those kids to this kind of music. I'd take the groups in. As soon as you'd take a group in and you'd get a hall that would hold 500 and you'd get 1,500 in it, and a lot of the kids in the audience who were musically inclined decided, "Hey, why don't we get together and form a group?" So you got a lot of groups.

The first group was called The Stripes. (Red always wore a trademark red and white striped sports jacket). There was another group called The Prowlers, which was named after Jack Cullen's show at the time. When the action started, he decided to go rock and he did it, I think, for three years.

McGrath: Are any of these musicians still around?

Red Robinson: Les Vogt is. He used to sing for The Prowlers, and now he runs *The Purple Steer* night club. But I never see any of the others—none of them went on to any kind of prominence. One guy did! One guy is very prominent today who was the lead singer of the original Stripes. We found him on the talent search, and his name is Ian Tyson. He's done all right.

McGrath: It's strange that there weren't more bands. The music wasn't difficult to play.

Red Robinson: That's right, but again—it's new. It's a new art form, and it was difficult to play because some of the kids who immediately wanted to do it were influenced by parents who may have come from the prairies and who were used to country music. You don't really have a large black community here, either.

McGrath: I guess instruments would be hard to find.

Red Robinson: Instruments, yeah. Try to find the right ones.

McGrath: Where would you get electric guitars and amps?

Red Robinson: You could get them, but the amps were the size of a small footstool. Little Fenders. But the talent thing really helped that. Seattle was the birthplace of a lot of the early west coast rock people, like The Fleetwoods. A lot of different groups, because rock went into five different starbursts.

It started from R&B—you can call it soul—it's grown and they've embellished it, but basically it's the same sound, and then you had "plastic rock," which was the whole era of the early 1960s with Fabian and Frankie Avalon and Bobby Rydell. There was really a lull, and it didn't get going again until the British said, Hey, we really like the hard stuff. The Americans were waltzing to Bobby Vinton.

Here's a little story I'll give you quickly in sequence— Buddy Holly was a fantastic influence on English kids. I had met Buddy here in 1957, at a big show at the old Denman Auditorium, which is now ripped down. As a matter of fact, where the old Denman Auditorium was is now the Four Seasons Hotel. I had played Buddy Holly's first record, *That'll Be The Day*, and it hit number one here for eight weeks and nobody was playing it in the US. Then it became a hit in the US and it worked in reverse, so when he came up I got to talk with him. Then he got killed in that plane crash in 1959. But his influence in England was fantastic. And basically, when I did The Beatles show here in 1964, I talked with John Lennon about Buddy's influence and John said that Buddy really did a lot for them. Even to the name. Anyway, The Crickets were on tour. Les Vogt and I had a booking agency and we toured the Crickets in 1963. Jerry Naylor and Sonny Curtis (members of the original Crickets) said listen to this record. It was called *From Me To You* and it was a hit for Del Shannon, so I said why should I? And he said the group that originally did it was really big in England and that I should get on it.

I was program manager at CFUN at the time. We played the record and about six months later nobody could even remember their names, and then six months after that *She Loves You* came out and the rest is history. What The Beatles provided, though, was the hard rock that was not being featured in North America. And it took the yanks about a year and a half to catch up.

McGrath: Right. I've thought about that trip, and it seems to me the difference between the sound of The Beatles and The Stones

Les Vogt and the Prowlers. Left to right: Les Vogt - vocals and guitar, Fred Bennett - lead guitar, Carl Ashley - drums, Larry Tillyer - bass, Carl Ries - sax.

and even The Dave Clark 5 was directly opposed to the self-centred, narcissistic adolescence of American pop songs. To me the Brits seemed extroverted in their sound.

Red Robinson: That's a good analysis. The Beatles included people other than teenagers. And by doing this, they solidified the listening audience—rock became cohesive again.

But this is getting away from it all. Let's go back to the radio show in 1954. The thing grows. I go out and do a remote broadcast from a shoe store which is advertised a week ahead. This is where you first get an indication that things are really happening.

It was at a place called Copp's Downtown Shoe Store, which is still there, next to Woodward's on Hastings. The show was supposed to start at four and by four everybody was crammed in the store. Six hundred people were crammed so tightly they broke the showcases. The line went up the stairs, all the way past Woodward's, all the way to Army & Navy (about three blocks). That's unreal. In those days you gave away records and it was a big thing. I guess it was because there really wasn't too much money around. So you'd hold up a 78 and smack!, goodbye, because they broke on contact. Sometimes just eye contact.

And from there, as the thing grew, it was a matter of taking the music to the people. I would go to the Orpheum Theatre and we'd run Saturday things. They'd run some movie like *The Lone Ranger Attacks an Indian Reserve in Thailand*, and everyone would go bletch and at the intermission you'd bring on the groups.

This is where we'd have a parallel thing going. Jack Cullen, who was the original disc jockey in town, was playing some rock and mixing it with the musical bag of the day: Frankie Laine singing *The Cry of the Wild Goose*, or Frank Sinatra singing *I'm Over 50 and I'm Retired* or whatever it was, and Jack, who was an enterprising guy, started booking acts in.

In 1956 he booked in Bill Haley. Then I'd go out and book a different group. Then someone else would do a different group. Finally, Cullen realized he was over the hill, so he gave it up and went back to being Jack Cullen. But good things happened to the public as a result. We saw and heard people like Earl Bostick, who played fantastic sax, and Chuck Berry and Little Richard.

We used to have problems, too. Up in City Hall is a statute that reads, if I can remember it, "Anyone under the age of 18 is not allowed to attend a public dance without the permission of—and this is where I get screwed up—or in company with, an adult over the age of 21."

What were you supposed to do? So we did it anyway, and, you know, you pay a $25 fine and all that jazz. Fortunately, we had a sort of neutral territory. We'd go to the PNE (Vancouver's summer fairgrounds), book the Forum or Gardens and get 2,000 to 3,000 out for a dance.

Somebody would always get into a fight with a beer bottle, which was always the thing, because some guy in a '55 Chev would see some nice 21-year-old girl, ask her for a date, and then her boyfriend would hammer him. That and trying to get too many people into a small joint.

McGrath: So did each DJ have his own group?

Red Robinson: Basically, yes.

Quigley: How did Jack Cullen get his group together?

Red Robinson: He ran a contest on the air. If you could sing H-A-Double-R-S-O-N Clothes, which was the jingle for a haberdasher who's no longer here, and sing it like a rock song, you won. They became The Prowlers and I think they won $5 and a piece of cloth.

Our group won a big trophy you could fill with gin. This is when I started the dances, and I couldn't hold them in Vancouver, so I went all over the Fraser Valley, anywhere where the bylaw didn't affect me. Then other groups started happening on their own. So instead of booking one group, I would alternate. People get tired of hearing the same band all the time. Pretty soon there were groups all over. Lots of these people are still around. Some very good guitar players came out of that, and I know it was an influence on the music. Garry Taylor used to be the drummer in a group call The

Classics which became the CFUN Classics, which became The Collectors, which became Chilliwack.

McGrath: What was the record scene like then?

Red Robinson: In those days I could get a record out if I paid for the mastering, which would probably be done at Al Rossh's studio, called Aragon Records. Then, you'd ship the master back east and have copies pressed and then sell them ourselves. That was the only way we could get records out. That's how Cullen got The Prowlers out on records. Records came out and they did all right, but in comparison to the material which was coming out of the US, it was pretty bad, because in reality it was a copy. But it inspired other groups to try other things.

McGrath: OK, so you left CJOR in 1957...

Red Robinson: Right. Then I went to CKWX. I'll tell you why. CKWX at the time was going to 50,000 watts and it would be the only station west of Winnipeg to have a 50,000 watt transmitter. And I saw a chance to let more people be exposed to the music of my generation.

So I went to 'WX in 1957 and again there was the situation of the unbelievable two-hour radio show. Within a year they converted 'WX into a the first 24-hour Top 40 station—although in those days in was Top 50. I met the man who converted 'WX in 1958. He was quite old at the time. I guess he was around 60 and he had great foresight. He was called Tiny Alfie, and he was big, around 6'5", and he said, "This is where it's gonna be at." Market research in the US showed that when people went into bars they played the same song again and again on the jukebox.

Tiny said, "Let's turn the station into a 24-hour jukebox." So Tiny took this multi-million dollar radio station, which was doing very well, and he made the decision that if rock was good enough for five hours a day, it was good enough for 24 hours. It was a huge success.

McGrath: What do you remember that was interesting or odd from those days?

Red Robinson: Everything ended in rhyme—stacks of wax and all that stuff. And we had cute little one-liners that today would be on T-shirts. They're funny when you look back, but they were serious at the time. For example—A greater measure of listening pleasure—pretty funny.

McGrath: Increase Records has released a series called A History Of Rock'n'Roll Radio. Have you heard them?

Red Robinson: Yes, I know the people who put that set together. It was fun. If you listen to old rock, you can tell it's not involved, which is probably a criticism today. But it was happy music and I don't think too many people got into the words. Probably you could interview 20 people on the street these days and only one would know the lyrics to any old song.

Quigley: Which station were you at when Elvis came to town?

Red Robinson: CKWX.

Quigley: Who was on CJOR after you left?

Red Robinson: They ran a contest (laughs). They had contests for everything. So they went to all the High Schools and they found Brian Forst.

McGrath: Who I knew as Frosty.

Red Robinson: He became Frosty only at CFUN. In those days he was Brian Forst, Boy DJ. He was on for five or six months and then the ratings came out and they realized they couldn't fight a 24-hour rock operation. He lasted six months and then he went to work in Prince George. So he was my replacement, but he couldn't make it, so CJOR went back to... what? They vacillated right up to 1964.

Those were the days when there was a fan cub, not for me, but for the show. Everything was a show. I had 55,000 members. They all had cards, and these became a merchandising tool. It was an advantage to the merchant, and everyone else who got one, because you could get discounts. And because we were going 24 hours a day, it stretched the teen thing to young adults, who previously wouldn't admit they liked this music. And then the younger kids started digging it. But it really went like a hydrogen bomb when the transistor radio came in. In 1959 I went to Portland to get into some television and I ended up at KGW radio in Seattle. I did a television thing and I lived there for two years and went into the US Army. I got a discharge and came back to town. Back to CKWX. But by that time, Tiny had died and they had lost the feeling. It turned really plastic—you know, 50-year-old guys playing rock.

They were nice guys but they just weren't with it. And it was too obvious. CFUN had started up in the summer of 1960 when I was in the army, and they played rock using young guys. Dave McCormick, Brian Forst, Hal Jordan—and they took it and got the momentum away from 'WX.

I worked for 'WX for a year, realized there was no hope, and then I had an offer from CFUN to go and be program director, so I went and stayed there. That was the greatest time, in my opinion, for rock. Those seven years I was there saw the music become a true art form. The guys there were young and aggressive and they created a lot of things, like the Soundathon, in which the 500 greatest records would be played for a whole long weekend.

Quigley: Was that idea original to Canada, or did it come from the US?

Red Robinson: Other stations had run Sound Spectaculars, but we were the first to have a Soundathon, with printed sheets of the top 500 songs we compiled from people's votes. No kidding, we'd get 50,000 pieces of mail that had to be tabulated.

We'd get 200 or 300 high school students to help us out. It was fun. It was exciting. We'd do anything. A week wouldn't go by without us holding up a train... anything for a gag. Then we started the Kits Showboat concerts, and this generated more talent.

The CFUN Classics. Left to right: Claire Lawrence - sax, organ, flute, Tom Baird - keyboards, Howie Vickers - lead vocals and trombone, Brian Russell - guitar, Gary Taylor - drums, Glenn Miller - bass.

McGrath: How did you get the CFUN Classics going? Another contest?

Red Robinson: (laughs) No. We were a bit more sophisticated. We went out and got who we considered to be the best guitarist, the best drummer, etc., and we brought them together and called them The Classics. No, actually, they picked the name.

Quigley: When did CKLG come along?

Red Robinson: September, 1964.

Quigley: What were they before? A talk station?

Red Robinson: No, they had everything. They had a great show called *My Favourite Dish*. Do you remember that? They had an Italian show and Horst Koehler—we called him Horse Collar—so they decided to go for broke.

McGrath: And they did...

Red Robinson: (laughs) And they brought a guy called Sam Holman in from New York.

Quigley: How did this affect you at CFUN?

Red Robinson: Initially, we died a thousand deaths—actually, there's always a part of your audience that's fickle. But nothing appreciable happened in the ratings until 1966.

McGrath: When they've got nothing to lose, they can usually start off being a tad more progressive and the established favourite.

Red Robinson: The novelty thing. They lasted but we actually gave it to them when CFUN had internal problems with the three guys who owned it. They lived in Welland, Ontario, and they left us alone. Usually. But all of a sudden they weren't getting along. So they sold the joint and divided the money up. And that, in effect, killed us. I quit in 1967.

McGrath: I have to ask about the Beatles concert and John Lennon. I was there, believe it or not, and I remember you coming out and telling everyone to sit down.

Red Robinson: Yes, the Beatles' concert. I wasn't even supposed to be there. I had chosen one of the station's deejays to do The Beatles show and at the last minute my guy comes down with mononucleosis, so I decided to do it. First there was the press conference and then the show started at a little after 8pm before over 20,000 fans.

Huge.

The lineup that night started with the Bill Black Combo, the Exciters, The Righteous Brothers and finally Jackie DeShannon. At around 9:30pm I went out on stage to introduce The Beatles. The noise was deafening. They did a couple of numbers—*Twist and Shout, You Can't Do That, All my Loving, She Loves You*— and the crowd was pushing forward to the makeshift stage that was setup.

The Chief of Police told me you have to stop this. Then Brian Epstein told me about English football games. When a lot of people push forward some people are going to get crushed and some could even die. Brian basically told me you have to go out there and tell the crowd if you don't back down the Beatles would quit and leave. I got up there on stage, waited for the end of a song and then I walked out.

As I passed John Lennon he looked at me and said, "Get the fuck off of our stage!" I asked John look at all the people at the foot of the stage and told him Brian had sent me up here because the crowd was getting out of control. John looked down and said, "Yeah. OK, carry on mate." So I talked to the audience. But that doesn't matter. (laughs) I will always be remembered as the guy John Lennon told to get the fuck off his stage.

High Flying Bird: We Love What We Do

Vancouver, May, 1972.

THE ALMOST-MADE-IT story is oft fraught with ennui, and in this interview with a successful local group of the era there is a sort of tired sense that their particular musical string may be tuning out. This piece was done in large part because my comrades in ink were growing a tad tired of my fascination with touring rock stars (ibid.) and wanted more of a local angle—which was a bit of a letdown after the verbal antics of, say, Captain Beefheart.

Never mind. High Flying Bird were a high-flying group. They amused fans in western Canada from 1969 to 1973, releasing two singles but no album. At their peak they did a number of opening act audience warm-up gigs for touring acts such as Jethro Tull, Ten Years After, Fleetwood Mac, Steve Miller, and a western tour with Willy Dixon. Not bad company. The original band was Barry Cartwright on drums, Rick McPhee on vocals, Charlie Bill Knowles on bass, Peter McLean on keyboards and vocals, and Brent Shindell on guitar and vocals. By the time of this interview Rick McPhee had left and Barry Cartwright had been replaced by Shawn Byrne on drums. When we talked The Bird had just returned from two weekend gigs on Vancouver Island, and a long tour with Willie Dixon through western Canada, stopping at Calgary, Nelson, Edmonton, Lethbridge, Victoria, Prince George, Penticton and Vancouver. Road band.

Here is the discursive article as published in *The Grape*:

Around seven I wandered in through the front door and into the Bird's nest. Lots of people and a great friendly dog are on hand to greet you, and before too long we were sprawled around the living room, talking bands and music. High Flying Bird was, in 1972, one of the older still-working rock groups in town, having carried on over three years and numerous personnel changes. At inception they had Brian McManus playing lead guitar, and then Brian changed his name and his thinking to Vanya Skye and the group became known around as a working extension of the Skye Family. When Vanya left and started Motherhood, the original Family died, but the basic philosophy of "people living together and loving each other" still lingers on in the house on Fremlin Street.

The first thing I wanted to cover was the Bird's interest in the local scene. What seemed to piss them off the most was the fact they couldn't get out and see the groups that they wanted to see—too many groups and nowhere for them to play.

I suggested the possibility of a number of groups getting together and doing a series of concerts or trying to open a club, but besides agreement on the fact that most promoters could easily be cut out of the music scene, thus giving the groups more of a chance to make some money, there was little optimism that such a scheme could get off the ground. The idea did stir up a few nostalgic stories, though, and the next thing I knew we were neck deep in "the good old days" and how it used to be when the Retinal Circus and the Bistro and everything else was going full tilt. Especially the Elegant Parlour, with its local legend sets featuring Brahmin or Stallion Thumbrock or The Seeds of Time.

When things finally got back to the present and I learned a new HFB single was soon to be released. The song is a Paul Williams number called *I Never Had It So Good* with lead vocals by Peter McLean (*a.k.a.* Zeke) and production by Tim Burge. The song was recorded locally at Aragon Studios.

Barry Samuels, HFB's manger, is very excited about the record and feels that it has a good chance to break the group on a national level. If that does happen, The Bird will be well on their way to doing an album of their own songs. Which shouldn't be too difficult, considering the present lineup has a repertoire of about 25 original tunes, and Brent Shindell (guitar) and Peter (keyboards) are currently both into writing. I asked how they got songs together and Shawn (drummer) answered: "Zeke writes a song—let's say he has the words and certain parts figured out, and we run through it and we all arrange it. Zeke has the basic idea and we just add parts, or maybe take a part out, and finally we end up with something that's done by four people. When Brent writes a song he comes in with a riff, and we just start working on that. And that turns into a song."

The conversation then shifts to a discussion of Canadian music. It has long been my contention (Poppy Family excluded) that the recording heavies in Canada have totally ignored the West Coast bands. Thunder Studios in Toronto seem to be the focus point for Canadian rock recording and even though there is an incredible amount of music coming out of that area—no doubt to appease the Canadian content and the even newer "Canada Sound" bullshit that rockers in the States are now getting flogged with—it appears that absolutely nothing has been done with the vast amount of music this town produces.

As Samuels says, "A band's success is a direct result or the audience. If the people are not hearing on the radio a representation of what is being created here, then they're going to be less prone to accept what's created here." There is another obstacle in the way of local music. If you belong to a group and you want to record a song, there are two ways you can do it: put up all the money and rent the studio time and do the thing.

Very expensive.

The other way is to try and get the studio or somebody to back you. Drummer Shawn Byrne explains: "All the studio time is up front—so say the record sells, well, then all the studio costs come off the top. After that's paid for then the group can start talking royalties and things."

One of the backlashes of this kind of system is that in most cases, like now, when money is tight, most bands—unless they have a super commercial sound or have taken advanced courses in mass hypnosis—can't get to do what they want in a studio. But music is not all Business & Bucks to a band, and High Flying Bird certainly don't treat music as a means to money.

The music holds much more meaning to them than that, according to Zeke: "What I want to do in my writing is try to think of a lot of things that might be beneficial if people know about it. Not just learning a bunch of things and writing them down. And not crashing them over the head with it, but doing it in a subtle way. Some things that may be a gas for people to learn. Move them somewhere."

As for the future, Shawn expresses the feelings of the Bird and a lot of other musicians when he says, "I don't concern myself too much with the future, as I don't concern myself too much with the past. If you were to look in my room you'd find only one nostalgic item—all that stuff about fame and fortune is just The Dream.

"When I go to a gig I see the stage and the drums set up on it. And I look upon it as a stage and we're an act and we have to get up and entertain those people for as long and as well as we can. When you're enjoying it, then it's a lot of fun. That's when I feel the best. If I have a whole day I'm feeling best when I'm sitting behind my kit rather than when I'm doing anything else.

"It's probably the same thing for anybody who plays anything. They just get high. Especially when I play free form stuff—but you can't do that at a gig because people aren't going to want to hear exactly what you're feeling right at that moment. So you have to put in the old two-quarter beat and stuff they can stamp their feet to. I don't mind that once I've had a few beers; I can get into it just as much as anyone. Which is what we usually do.

"When we play at dances everyone's usually drunk or they're hootin' and hollerin'—so to make the dance successful we drink a little ourselves to get that rapport with the audience. And we're jumpin' up and down and hootin' an hollerin' and they're doing the same and it's a successful dance. Everybody goes home after having a good time and they say 'Wow, they were great!'—but we don't say that, we say we weren't so great—we were sloppy, but the people were satisfied.

"It's mainly the feel of the music that comes across. You wish the audience could be a little looser in their heads so that they could do it to just about anything. A lot of people can do it to any kind of music but there are people who need to clap their hands four times to be able to dance."

I asked them if they found this frustrating, and the evening and the interview ended with this thought. "The frustration could get really big. Right now it's really small. Like it's accepted, so we still get into doing high school gigs when we play them and we try to please the audience.

"It's not as though it's really hated. It's accepted because we have to do it in order to live. With us, it's like Motherhood—there's a lot of work out parts that you can't really stomp your foot to, it's mainly to listen.

"And people, maybe they don't like it, maybe what we're doing doesn't appeal to people in general, but it's our music and it's what we love to do."

Luke Gibson: After The Apostles

Vancouver, June 7, 1972

A COUPLE OF WEEKS AGO I saw a Vancouver concert given by one of the first influential Canadian blues singers, Luke Gibson. Luke was involved in what was the neophyte Toronto blues band, Luke and the Apostles, and after seeing that group fold just as it was peaking, he moved on to playing rhythm guitar and singing for the Kensington Market, one of the legendary progressive rock groups to emerge from the early Yorkville scene.

The Market, and their sister group, The Paupers, shone on brightly for a couple of years, and their eventual demise seemed to parallel the commercialization of the Yorkville flowering. I met Luke before the CKLG FM concert he did, and found him at first impression to be a rather quiet, introspective personality. He played well over the air, and after that gig we went back to his hotel room for a few beers and a talk.

Rick McGrath: Tell me what you remember about the Yorkville scene in Toronto.

Luke Gibson: It was fantastic. Really, really fuckin' great. It was so new. The clubs were like old houses and all these funky old buildings. It was just shoulder-to-shoulder jammed with kids every night. And this was just when people were just starting to grow their hair long—it was that whole social thing. And everyone was just getting stoned.

When we started playing there we were the only band there, and we used to get lineups down the street every night. We used to play there six nights a week during the summer and make five bucks a man.

McGrath: Chicago blues?

Luke Gibson: Yeah, we were just thumpin' away.

McGrath: You were into harp then, not guitar?

Luke Gibson: Yeah, I stood up and sang. One thing, though, was the incredible number of bands. That's when Neil Young was hanging out in an orange raincoat sitting on steps playing and Steppenwolf were the Sparrow and John Lee & The Checkmates became Rhinocerous, and Bruce Palmer—who else? Everybody was there.

McGrath: Was the musical community very close?

Luke Gibson: Very tight. There used to be a restaurant where we all hung out.

McGrath: Toronto is situated in a bowl of major American musical centres. Was there any influence say, from Chicago or Detroit or New York?

Luke Gibson: New York was about the most important place.

McGrath: Was it the place that Toronto musicians tried to get to?

Luke Gibson: Yeah, that was where you went. We went there with Elektra's Paul Rothchild. You won't believe this, like, we went to New York —we didn't have visas, right, so this is our first time, goin' to New York, and we were just freaked right out. And so we're all dressed up in our band clothes and our fucking hair and everything and we went to the airport and they caught us because we didn't have visas and they wouldn't let us in. You can imagine the disappointment—we were due in New York the next day—so we went home and dug around and got all our old suits out from our high school days and grease cuts, and wore these old straight suits. And we went back to the airport, and we looked much more bizarre than we had before, and they caught us again. But then eventually they let us go through, so everything was cool.

McGrath: Have you ever given any thought to the fact that you're a Canadian musician?

Luke Gibson: Oh yeah, I always have thought about that. For one thing, I ain't gonna get drafted. Frankly, I hate the States. I know there's great people there and I've got a lot of friends down there, but the overall trip that goes on there, well, I don't want to go near it. I've seen enough of that. It's the most violent country I've ever imagined. It's in the air—you can see it. Canada is really clear, like you can see the difference. When you fly up, as soon as you land and you get off the plane, you just see more, because the air's clearer, and I don't mean pollution, I mean vibes. It really is a lot nicer and it's because Canada isn't on a fuckin' power trip. And I think people in Canada are smart enough and aware enough so that they're not going to do that. The only trouble with getting on a heavy nationalistic trip is the waving flags and the power number. It's good to have a fuckin' identity.

McGrath: What do you think about the fact that Canada's aiding the US in Vietnam and the fact that English soldiers and tanks are training in Alberta?

Luke Gibson: I don't go for that—either of them. I think we should be more like Switzerland. I think Switzerland is as neutral as you can get it. I don't think we should endorse any kind of violence.

McGrath: You were involved in a trip over an airport...

Luke Gibson: There's an area about thirty miles outside of Toronto, and it's a rural area, and what they wanted to do was expropriate the whole strip and build a fuckin' airport there. Not only that, but they'll have to build a freeway out to it. I could see why these people wanted to fight it, because I wouldn't want an airport built where I live. People should just slow down a bit. We don't need more airports. We don't have to run around that much, we really don't. They're just driven mad by business and making money and everything. And money's all right, and so is business, but it's just such a fucking dominant thing in everybody's head that it's all they're into: it's like a god.

McGrath: I suspect that's why you live the way you do...

Luke Gibson: That's it—I don't want no part of it. I have to make money and I don't mind making money for what I do—but I don't make it without reason. Because I don't need it. People think they need so many things and they really don't. People are totally dictated by television.

How to think, what to wear, what to spray on, what to shove up their ass. If I can see that, and I'm no smarter than anybody else as far as I can see, I've got the same brain as everybody else, what freaks me out is why can't people see through that bullshit. It's just bullshit and they're just fuckin' themselves up. And they're turned into fuckin' robots.

McGrath: Yeah, but all you have to do is look out those windows (we're on the 7th floor of the Mayfair Hotel) and those kind of things don't enter into the minds of people caught in this kind of environment.

Luke Gibson: I guess some people just go along with it and think that's what's real. Where I live I don't even have electricity. I shut it off. There it's just a different world. It's like in *Black Elk Speaks*. Did you ever read that?

McGrath: No.

Luke Gibson: It's narrated by a Sioux holy man and it was written in the 30s or 40s. This guy went up a mountain in Dakota where this Black Elk was living. And some of his friends were there and they were still alive and they had been at Big Horn and Wounded Knee and they told this story in this book.

McGrath: I've tried to read Bury My Heart at Wounded Knee, but it's pretty heavy, I'd like to read something about the Canadian Indians.

Luke Gibson: The only thing around is a pamphlet put out by the Department of Indian Affairs which is a total fuckup history book. It reads like a Grade Seven history book. It goes like: So-and-so, Lord Uggabugga, introduced flugabug and encouraged the fur trade, blah blah blah and then we shot them all and blugga blugga and then influences of Catholicism and Protestantism and ugga bugga, But to get back to that book. They were talking about wanting the gold in the Dakota hills. And Black Elk says, "The white man thinks there is some of the yellow metal in our hills. The yellow metal that they worship and it makes them crazy." They really knew.

McGrath: What differences are there in your style between the old Luke and what you're into now?

Luke Gibson: It's easily equated to the difference in miles between Vancouver and Toronto. It's light years away.

McGrath: What do you see the two thing representing?

Luke Gibson: Well, music is music, for one thing, and the basic feel of playing music is fairly constant. And the things that I learned in Luke and The Apostles I've retained. And so that's still in my songs, even if it sounds like country. From the Apostles I went from just basic, well, music, to the Market with things like melody and dissonance and now it's all sort of come home. To the point that I'm just sitting and playing myself.

McGrath: One thing I've noticed is the fact that you tend to express yourself musically and lyrically within a certain set of images and image patterns. Do you pick up on these from your environment?

Luke Gibson: Yeah, some songs are about people and some are about being free and some are about being hung up. A lot are about nature.

McGrath: Do you think it's a Canadian artist's trip to first think of expressing himself in environmental imagery?

Luke Gibson: Probably, yeah, I think that's always been predominant among Canadian writers.

McGrath: Do you see it as part of a Canadian artist's search from some kind of self identity?

Luke Gibson: No, I just think that's what they get off on. That's another thing—people are so afraid of Nature. If it snows or something, people think something is wrong. People are so fucked up.

McGrath: Nature is usually seen by man as something to overcome.

Luke Gibson: People think it's something to fight. That's what's wrong. Because they relate so much to fighting: fight, fight, fight.

McGrath: What do you think about the dramatic increase in Canadian music? Do you see it as having much to do with the CRTC? [Canadian Radio and Television Commission.

Luke Gibson: It seemed to me to be simultaneous. It seemed that everyone was building good recording studios.

McGrath: I find that interesting, because Ritchie Yorke was out here and he tended to let everyone believe that it was the CRTC that instigated all the activity.

Luke Gibson: Well, Neil Young and David Briggs built Thunder before that, and then they sold it.

McGrath: What do you think of the CRTC?

Luke Gibson: Well, the whole way the radio stations operate is a weird trip to me. You know—playlists and dictatorship and that trip. It's a fucking business or I don't know what it is. It's strange to me.

McGrath: Yeah, stations play songs that are hits but they're hits because they play them.

Luke Gibson: I don't understand it. Because all the smaller radio stations are dictated by the larger ones, and who the fuck says what's played? Who is that guy? It's weird.

McGrath: It's the old Canadian problem all over again. One of the criticisms I've heard about the CRTC is that they made the rules to get American bands off the air, and now it's replaced with Canadian bands sounding like American bands. Or Canadians on American labels.

Luke Gibson: That's why I believe in small companies.

John Lyle: Stone Blown From The Sky

Vancouver, June 8, 1972

HERE'S ANOTHER SEMI-INTERVIEW with a Vancouver musician who, like High Flying Bird, came agonizingly close to fulfilling their musical dreams. I first met John Lyle (*a.k.a.* The Singing Postman) when we were both university students, writing record reviews for the student newspaper. A few years later he released an album with very interesting songs, and so off I go to listen and write a review/introduction about John for *The Grape* newspaper. By 1980, after gigging around clubs and folk festivals, John had stopped performing live, gave up on the lifestyle, and decided to become a postman. He's now retired, but is still writing and recording songs today.

The Lost Guitar Interview.

Sunday night and the rain is just dogging down outside my room, my sloppy old room, and even as I write this line my mind is stretching out in front of me, paradoxically to the past of last week, when I sat in an old living room on the top floor of an old apartment block on Broadway and listened, really listened, to a poet called John Lyle who puts his words to music, himself to melody, and a bassist called Derek who plays the sweetest mellow lines to the ones I've already mentioned and even though I've only heard them once and likely won't hear them again for awhile, I left that old apartment different from when I entered and I guess that's probably because of what John the poet told me and what Derek the bassist felt and nothing to do with songs like *Blasted In Hope* which I think is as good a set of lyrics as Sweet Baby James can come up with now and again and it's all about, for me, at least, that:

Sweet low down and all around
The lone star whistle blows,
I've been trying to make connection
With my fast and lonesome Dixie flyer
Stream-lined and winding-fire,
stone-blown from the sky
To what's behind our lost tomorrows, baby

...and if our tomorrows are lost then what's behind them are our todays and if you feel like train has passed you by you got the blues and if you're trying to sing and write and eat you've also got the blues but they may be different because John Lyle was born in Flin Flon and that's in Manitoba and it all happened in 1946 along with the rest of us and "the next day" John told me "that I remember having any fun is the first day I picked up my Flamenco banjo and began banging out the *Bent City Blues*" and I lit a smoke and John said: "If you bang out the *Bent City Blues*, you're gonna want to bang out the *Bent City Blues* to the multitudes, and already you're in a lot of trouble. And when representatives of a cross-section of a corner of the multitudes become your friends, and they tell you they like your *Bent City Blues*, you're primed for a True Blue drowning" and if you caught that word "primed" you're ready to understand a bit of the basis behind John's version of the blues, his blues, country-western inspired blues that picks you up in homespun, wraps you in images and sets your mind on the back of a horse, or as a horse, as in:

I wish that l was one of Katharine Rosses hosses
We'd ride the range to the silver strains of me;
She'd ride astride and I'd feel obliged to wander
Wherever she might want the range to be.

> *Can't you see me now? I ain't no plow horse;*
> *I'm a saucy tossy Ross horse with my mistress*
> *Mounting me so bold and free*
> *And if my libido's showin', bet your spurs*
> *That I will be a growin'*
> *Palomino, pal of mine, you're gonna do me proud*

and the song goes on and the images flicker into life as you read them or hear them and they pile up, in a cumulative fashion, partly because of the space/time restrictions of an aural medium and partly because of their connotative progressions and suddenly you're left looking at yourself the same way John looks at himself: "A limited company of lost souls isn't the way to describe the crowd I run with, but it comes to mind—it's difficult not to manipulate, and it's even more difficult to manipulate positively—that writing and singing songs for people is my way out, but without acceptance and recognition my way out becomes another blockade and I really believe I don't get anything I don't deserve" and somehow back in that old faded living room the drifting got to roots and bands and I guess it all started for real for John back in 1967 with a funky little folk-rock band called the Gordian Knot that featured John and another musician called Gary (Deadly Certain) MacPherson and Gary had this girlfriend who was in love with him and her daddy was a California businessman and he and a few of his business buddies got together $100,000 to make the Knot into the Monkees so Gary blew off the girl and then it was 1969 with the Country Western Band—"Music that's kind to your mind"—and they gigged at Aldergrove and the Big Mother and the Bistro and just when the band started cooking Deadly Certain won a scholarship to study at Cambridge and he left but he knew "We could always write and sing, but it's taken so goddamn long to learn to play and arrange" and then after that there was a recording and writing contract with John Christian, Neil J. Godin and their outfit called Ocelot Records and John says, "I shoulda known from the name, but I get pretty hungry and basically they sat on me like I was a whoopee cushion, so I got out just before they fell apart" and then John picked up with Derek Stephanson—"mellowest bass player in Vancouver"—and practiced and wrote until this year when he met Robert Altman's daughter Christine Johnson and she led him "inside the golden circle to get a look at what I had considered to be the brass ring" and Altman heard him and had him sing three Leonard Cohen songs for his movie, *The Presbyterian Church Wager*, and then decided to use Cohen instead of John but offered to try and obtain a Warner recording contract which now boils down to Van Dyke Parks apparently trying to do something with one of John's tapes and even Lou Adler wants one and the song *Keep the Banners Flying* is a bit of a response:

> *My heart's been sent to Heaven*
> *and the same old used to be*
> *Still lingers on beside the riverside*
> *that holds a line on me*
> *The dream is an illusion and it never comes again*
> *Until the ocean tries to take you back*
> *to where you've always been*
> *And when the cave on Sugar Mountain*
> *is the only home*
> *I count on, I'm a fool; and when the grave beneath*
> *Death Valley is my mind inside an alley, I'll be cool*

and even disregarding John's love for Randy Newman and Jesse Colin Young and the Beatles and Neil Young and of course Bobby Dylan there is an influence, perhaps unknown to him, that stretches back to the sodbustin, goodtime music of Flin Flon which is in Manitoba and moving forward takes it all in, from the funk of early Van Morrison through Procol Harum and the Beach Boys until it reaches the present and even if you disregard all this you know he's made up of everything he's experienced and when you talk about rock and roll you know you've experienced it, too, even if we find it difficult to talk about, and the images he uses we can recognize way back in our heads and sometimes he gets it right "to feed the great mistake of intellect, the saving grace of soul" without hardly any effort at all:

> *If the steel insane insistent rain*
> *From my old lost guitar*
> *Can be a groove for me, a tune for you*
> *Help me raise the bar*

and when John picks up that lost guitar and plays a bit you want to help him along, you listen to his guitar talking, you hear his soft, high voice, his crazy words and you feel his desire to communicate spreading out and filling the room, your mind, and he runs a hand through his blonde hair and grins and sings:

> *Fair haired boys don't make no noise,*
> *No waves, no sudden moves.*
> *Fair-haired boys got ice-cold ploys,*
> *They use for mavin' smooth.*
> *And when circumstance combines with chance*
> *To make me on the move,*
> *I kill my schemes with gentle dreams that*
> *disprove what I prove.*

and it all comes together with the melody line that I can't express on paper and even if I could it would be a small substitute for the real thing and if there's nothing else I can say about John Lyle it's he was real and is real because he's putting it all together right now and biding his time but soon, Vancouver, soon he'll be telling us our secrets:

> *When our trust is in the gambler*
> *and the odds are on the wall*
> *And all the whores can beg for rain-checks*
> *while their johns lose all recall,*
> *And when our minds are always busy*
> *mailing letters to the sea,*
> *It's the show-off age and the show-off stage*
> *And the showdown might be tragedy*

and that's the first verse of *The Showdown Might Be Tragedy* which John wrote as the title song of *Presbyterian Church Wager* and even so, even so, you can dig it.

Al Neil: Cosmic Klangfarben

Art: Kerry Waghorn

Cates Park, North Vancouver, December 4, 1972

THIS WAS A VERY UNUSUAL choice of interviews—I wasn't much of a jazz critic and my only prior knowledge of Al Neil was his novella, *Changes*, which *The Straight* had run as a serial during 1970. A local Vancouver legend, both for his music and his self-publicized heroin addiction, Al proved to be an incredible interview, not the least for his high-powered energy level, no doubt assisted by various forms of amphetamines.

Early Days.

Alan Douglas Neil dropped into this world's existence in 1924 at Vancouver's General Hospital. His mother took him home to Main Street where he busied himself with the art of growing up. When Al reached nine years of age he started piano lessons under the aegis of Glenn Nelson, continuing his studies until 1940, when the fascist hordes made a break for power. Al turned to surveying and moved up to Hardy Bay, working for the Department of Transport. He helped make a runway—and then found himself in England, plotting tangents for the Army's artillery and surviving D-Day.

Johnny came marching home and Al came with him, armed with energy and itching to ascertain for himself the stories about the new jazz he had read in the war issues of *Downbeat* his mother had mailed to Europe.

Technique had to come first, so Al renewed his piano lessons with Nelson, Jean Couthard and others. It was Wilf Wylie, however, who first introduced Al to the joys and power of jazz piano. Books and scores were impossible to pick up in those days, so Al did the next best thing: old 78's played endlessly gave up their secrets to his discerning ear. Al was soon into the structures and harmonies of the likes of Charlie Parker, Dizzy Gillespie and Bud Powell.

"There was a point about 1947", says Al, "when some of us got tired and frustrated of not having a place to play. So we got together and formed a little society. In British Columbia you can get a charter that doesn't necessitate getting things like expensive yellow urinals and commissaries of various descriptions. You can just set up and get to work."

It was a move that ultimately changed Al's life and brought into being the heaviest jazz spot on the West Coast: The Cellar Jazz Club. Al set himself up and was the leader of the house band. "First there was the Al Neil Trio and then people like Don Thompson came in, along with two of the heaviest Alto players, still the best in Canada: Dale Hillary and P.J. Perry. He's still around.

"Most of us had jobs, you see. I was working in the Post Office and so we didn't need to take out too much bread. We slowly started getting into the Musician's Union and so on, but we had an arrangement with them so there was no hassle. If we had made $15 we'd take out five or ten and kick the rest back into the Club. It was several years before we paid ourselves the Union scale.

"So we were able to build up a kitty, and when we did well, we thought we'd start to bring in people from LA. Some of us were mildly interested in what was known as West Coast Jazz. So we started bringing in people like Barney Kessel, Conte Condali, Carl Fontana, Bill Perkins, Sonny Redd and Art Pepper as singles. And my rhythm section, or somebody else's rhythm section would play with them.

"One guy who was up here three times was Art Pepper. He's now doing thirty years. Bill Perkins was really impressed with us and he said there was a tenor player, a guy who blew something like Zoot Sims or Getz or one of those Lester Young derived musicians, but good, who showed up in LA from Texas. His name was Ornette Coleman and he had Don Cherry with him and Charlie Haydn on bass and Billy Higgins on drums. Perkins told us about them and just on the strength of his word we wrote and asked them to come up.

"They'd been getting booted out of all the clubs they'd played at, especially Ornette. He put in his dues. So they came up and it was their first fuckin' jazz gig in Vancouver, 1958. And they played here a week or ten days and just blew our fuckin' minds. We were there, six to eight hours a night, every night, just listening to them.

"Up until then we just had the West Coasters and these guys were playing New York jazz. Even the West coast blacks weren't into it. Miles Davis was seduced into those early albums with Gerry Mulligan, which apparently now he considers bullshit. Lots of heavy harmony but pretty lightweight energy, and they led into the three records he made with Gil Evans and the big band. Apparently Miles has just recently put those down as being bullshit, too.

"Then Harold Land came up two or three times and Ornette came back and Cherry lived here for two or three months. He lived with Dave Quarin, who is now an executive with the Musician's Union, and I don't know what he's doing for music. Cherry scared the shit out of all of us, he tried to form up a band, but we could only play the bebop stuff and he was already way past that. It took us ten years to get the bebop stuff down around here because everything was slower. And Cherry comes along and he thought he could move us up a notch. We just weren't ready for it. A bunch of us were starting to get fucked up on dope, too. I got out of that.

"I copped out around 1962. I figured I had had enough and I was starting to hear stuff that couldn't be played in the harmonic structure we were using. I was going crazy because I could hear it and if I tried to play it Hillary would turn around and say "Play the fuckin' changes," because if I played what I was hearing I would fuck up the rhythm section and the horn players.

"One night I took a trumpet player from LA and I heard this solo and I thought, well, I'm going to screw up the rhythm section so I just played it on the wall on my head. The wall was right behind me. Quarin, who was manager at the time was really upset. At the intermission he was getting heavy with me at the bar and the trumpet player turned around and said he thought it was a good solo. I figured I had to get out of there anyhow, and the next year I was out delivering handbills on the street."

Besides Cherry, Coleman, *et al*, Al and the Cellar saw the likes of Scatt Ja Faro, Elmo Hope, James Clay, Monty Waters and many more 50's greats who set down in Vancouver in their movement from one gig to the next.

Al was, along with the Cellar regulars, a familiar musician to the radio and TV audiences of Vancouver, as well as writing scores for NFB movies. Stardom glinted momentarily with a tour Al did with American poet Kenneth Patchen that culminated in an album he and Patchen recorded for Folkways records in New York.

But that was it.

Al jumped back to Vancouver to help the late Barry Cramer in his early stage productions of Beckett, Ionesco, and Arrabel and then, in 1962 Al did what few people would dare: he found the courage to shut out junk, his music, his friends and associates and begin his life over. Working at the most menial of jobs, Al kept to himself and immersed his being in private study, mostly metaphysical.

Human relations came back, as they must, and after two years of retreat and meditation Al eventually began working with Gregg Simpson and Richard Anstey, searching out new expressions of jazz. Contact with Sam Perry, Gary Lee Nova, Dallas Selman and others resulted in the formation of Intermedia. The music had returned.

Al, Gregg Simpson and Marguerite Neil began touring,

giving concerts in Edmonton, Regina, Toronto, Kingston and Halifax over several seasons.

This year another aspect of Al Neil has been made public. The Vancouver Art Gallery hosted its first one man show of art objects, music, slides and movie videos, as Al showed all facets of his creativity for the first time in a month-long exposition which lasted from March 14 to May 14 of 1972.

Two books, *West Coast Lokas*, published by Vancouver Community Press, and a novel, *Changes*, published by Coach House Press of Toronto, have also appeared.

Over the Volcano.

Al lives out by Cates Park in a ramshackle old houseboat—a renovated barge—that clutters the beach a shot away from the cabin in which Malcolm Lowery drank and agonized *Under The Volcano* from his typewriter. Like Lowery's metaphorical retreat, "Las Chivas," Al's retreat strikes the observer as being at once a junkyard of "accumulated life and things" and yet a new spark, a flame fanned by the energy force that inhabits it.

Just as Al's house becomes a houseboat when the tide is high, so does the visitor undergo transformation: from the road to the beach house is a hundred yards of three-hundred-year-old cedar giants, branches washed in rain and roots deep in the earth. They're like a grove of giant spines up and down whose length shiver pre-primal statements in sympathy with the watery pounding of the waves and the snare-drum pebbles of the beach below. The wind shrieks and moans, blowing like some crazy on horn and in the midst of all this is Al, stoking the fire, burning his memory of musical conventions, and trying to restate the feeling in his gut on the 56 keys of his piano that still sound to the touch of his fingers.

It's as if Al has been able to cleanse his mind at the expense of his immediate spatial surroundings: the junk, the things, the objects, the crap of his mind has been lessened while, like some great metaphysical balance, the garbage index of his surroundings has increased in equal proportion. One comes close to the house and one enters a strange world of decay, of rusted bits of metal, of old pieces of this, of broken hunks of that, some of it strung together, some of it mashed into frames with broken pieces of glass intensifying the effect and mirroring the junk piled around it.

And being junk, it's all smashed, useless, destroyed; it is also, one realizes, arranged... a fantastic collage of things that assault the person in their rottenness but at the same time teach, in a political sense, the corporate sense of art as object. Art objectified becomes junk in museums. Art objectified becomes trash on display. Art objectified ties up Magic and puts it into the Aristotelian linear spatial baggie of Western duality and, after securing the top with its own twistie, puts it in a can till the trashman comes and takes it away. The Dadaists tried to break the bag so they made the bag bigger and included the Dadaists. Al Neil waited at the dump. He may save them all.

What Al Neil is (not does) is Art Subjectified. Al neither listens nor produces: Al is Art. So am I. So are You.

Inside the house, five of us, a good number for Al, and he's alive and swinging with the tape recorder on. Towards the end of the talk a question goes out concerning Al's plans for the

future. The answer comes: "No, I'm not hoping. If you hope, that means a future and it's situated right here on my two feet. What I'm doing is consolidating everything I've done in the past twenty-five years, which has always been the same thing, and if I get this grant it means I'm going to be travelling a little bit. I've a whole new life opened up to me because I feel different inside. Everybody's noticed it, all my friends. If I can go backwards a little bit, it was when my ego was having something to rub up against, namely a ying-yang system of male/female that I couldn't figure out. And when that disintegrated, I found out slowly there was no hostility, no aggressiveness, except against pigs or Nixon or somebody objectified that way around the Planet. So I began to get higher and higher, and I defined it, that it was down through the sex chackra that all the suffering and pain, just like Buddha says, started.

"And that's where all my hostilities, emotional and psychic, and sometimes physical, all my violence against the woman I loved, started. When that drifted apart, and we're getting back to now, and when I start a new relationship I'm not getting back into that. And I'm lucky because I'm so fucking high l just refuse to come down into that. It's gotta be amazing, you see. So my plans are to keep my body in good shape... l have to remember to keep eating. Really, you know if you read *Changes* you know I've been through that drug scene and I just have to keep remembering to keep eating. I just can't believe it. I'm shooting the energy right where I need it, and where I want it.

"So I got my body connected up OK. I got my new spectacles here and it gives me 20-20 vision and I'm just about to become a welfare bum. Permanently. A guy came down here from the rehabilitation centre and he saw me making one of my head things and he said: "l don't want to embarrass you, Al, but I just recommended you be listed unemployable." (laughs) So I got a pension, brother. I'm going to get new teeth out of it.

"Then next year I'm going to travel around and get out what I've got up to this date and show Ornette and those guys that might've remembered me and, you know, no ego trips, just to show them that there's high energy out here in the Rain Forest and somebody got something together, you know.

"And the next step for the rest of my life is to form up these Mandalas. In whatever system, because that's what I'm doing and they're infinite. It would be with visual, aural and whatever other, chanting, you know, it's infinite. Jack Wise knows that. I tried to find him yesterday but he's peddling his mandalas for $1200 apiece and when I went over there to find him yesterday the lady in the gallery (laughs) said he's gone to get some visual aids. And I said fuck, he doesn't need any visual aids. It turned out he needed them to drive his car whenever he goes to town.

"He (Wise) knows what he's doing. He's just tightening up his form.

"I happened to stumble into a system of kundalini by some rare conjunction of events, which are too dangerous for me to reveal. And this is true and this is not hype. I'll see how many tips I can give. One, is that I set out myself to give, or find, like I thought any man should, thanks to my mother, who's 90 years old right now and she's completely stoned and high on God, and a mystic. She's an opera singer from Massey Hall in Toronto from the turn of the century, and she's so fuckin' high she has to wear dark glasses to avoid the White Light. But there's a conjunction of that setting out as your destiny before you, which I did twenty years ago in a magazine in this City called *P.M.*, in two articles. One was called *Art and Mysticism* and the other was *The State of Consciousness in Jazz*. And so it was the conjunction of my mother's influence and having that destiny already spelled out for me, which I could do nothing about.

"The second thing was this: I chose to study two forms of spirituality, and there are hundreds, thousands, to get into the unity and the integration. Astrology, or whatever way you're going to do it.

"The two I chose were Zen, for its humour, and Tibetan, for its kundalini. The third element is too dangerous for me to reveal, but it happened to me by accident. Somebody performed something on my body by accident. And because of studying Tibetan Buddhism, I knew I was into it. I couldn't have gotten into it just by reading a book on Buddhism, but I knew I was into it.

The fourth thing was drugs. But the third thing, the one I'm hesitating to reveal, it concerns the seed. And so I was lucky enough to conjunct all this together and realize what the Tibetans were talking about. And I can't reveal this to anybody and there's no need to, because everybody's got to find their own way up into the triangles of reintegration, the return to God. And that's why you're feeling what I have to say to you and— that's what I have to give. It's not me that's giving it, it's someone else.

"And that's no fuckin' hype.

"It's there, it's there, and I can't deny it. And I'm scared. I'm fuckin' awestruck, man. I'm awestruck.

"The fifth thing, I just thought of. Since New Year's Day of last year when my wife left and the three months of the duality pain was over, I noticed I was going up. And I reasoned this way: the pain that I had been suffering through three eight year marriages was in the duality and the sex chackra and I felt myself getting higher and higher and higher. And when I had a brief romantic fling, and we mutually declared ourselves Platonic after the fourth bout in my bed, (laughs) because she fell out of it. (Al's bed is four feet above floor level)

Anyway, and this is the clue, and we get to the secret number, five: celibacy. If you know what you're doing with it, you can get the triangles upward. Celibacy. And this is still duality, it's between the sensuality and the aestheticism. And if you're working with extremes, it's still Duality, but it's better to get it up into the heart and the head and the possibility of opening up the suture on the top of your head than it is to go downward into the darkness of duality. Into everything that fucks up man and woman. Yin Yang is a sex chackra. Down is duality, disintegration, up is the apex thru the *axis maundi* of the spine to the axis of the earth pole star and on out."

Electric Entropy.

A pause from this subject and soon we're off on another line: Al's new album, which is soon to be released. Al puts down electricity as using up energy, and is asked how he feels this will affect his own album, going, as it must, through several degrees of electric entropy.

"Then we have to get into the media of feeding it through

electricity and what we're talking about is spirituality. It comes down from the Creator through the Solar System down in through you and if it turns into electricity then the electricity cancels out a lot of the energy.

"The media, from VTR to tape recorders and everything else, I'm giving it all up. And when I get some bread next year I'm going to get short wave radio, I'm not going to reveal... yeah... Stockhausen has given me the first energy that anybody has for ten years.

"I'm going to get one sound source, the best possible short wave radio l can get. A Halicrafter. Because it's picking up all the sounds in every language that are going around the globe. And maybe some coming in from outside, eh? And maybe I'll get some twelve year old genius to figure out some dimensions on fucking with it. But I can't deal with synthesizers or moogs or any of those because they're such low energy sound.

"And by low energy, I mean if you have a note, a pitch, aaaaaaaaaah (sings) that's the pitch of the Moog. But if you have it coming from the creator into the *axis mundi* (and returning) it's aaAhhaaaHHHAHAHaaa and that energy is the particles or klangfarben around the note and it includes the room and the ambiance of the room and the people in the room.

"And when that's fed through the electricity it comes out as a metallic aaaaaah right back where you started from. So the best possible thing you can do, like if I get this record out, is get a good grand piano. That's why the electronics just kills everything.

"And I'm going to do it to the VTR boys. Haven't you ever seen yourself on TV? Just this deathly grey dot plane. And you're always brought down. I was playing all through the 50's on CBC television. Art Pepper and everything. I kept it to myself because it was an intuition then, but I always thought we did really great, and then there's a whole room full of people. Some negative and some positive.

"Some people don't like you, the electricians or whatever, and you're trying to get this great fucking thing on and Art Pepper comes in and he's stoned on junk and we've already planned our program and it's ten minutes before the TV show goes on and he throws down something new he thought up on his junk dream and l had to try and figure out how to read it in ten minutes and the producer's getting nervous and it turned out really high energy and it's beautiful. And then you watch it played back and there's this little twenty inch square of grey dots and all you can see is nothing.

"That's why I'm going to use the Halicrafter. Because I can't get enough out of the $10,000 Steinways to please me. In the next year or two I'm going around on my own. I've been working on my own. On the 88. I'm going to use the Halicrafter for other collage systems. I'm going to be looking for people who are situated in music like I am. Stockhausen's found five. He's got his group together. They're tuning into the short wave and that's why I say he's given me the energy. I'm going to be writing to him because I know what I'll do with it is completely different from him and his Russian-Germanic polyglot system that he's arrived into.

"It's a sound system. Instead of having the moog synthesizer you have a Halicrafter radio. So instead of hearing beep beep beep, which is manufactured by the system, the same system we're trying to defeat, and not only because it's got no energy because they're pure sounds, they're sine tones.

"Sine means they've got no energy because it's pure. I can't do it with my voice. The most obvious example of their corruption is the sounds they make for that guy who made the Bach out of it. That's the most vulgar, stupid thing that anybody ever did.

"With the Halicrafter, what you hear when you tune it in is a foreign language, (or other sound) so you'll be able to chant to it because it's just coming in as a sound, and those people might be saying 'Look out, there's a fucking bomb coming down' and it's a sound source. Stockhausen, he's worked with synthesizers and with short wave radio. The only thing is that I'll do it completely different. He sits away out and he feeds it through a bunch of echoes and stuff while the musicians sit down there. He's still chairman (fascist.) I'm going to be sitting in the centre, not because of the ego, but because I'm a medium and I'll let it flow through with five musicians sitting around me, and I know how to write for them now, and I'll tie it all together.

"But it won't be 'I' tying it. Stockhausen still thinks he's tying it together, because he still sits away back and his five musicians sit down there and each one has a short wave radio and he's told sound comes up he's told them ten or fifteen ways to relate to that sound. But he sits back, and takes what they've done and then he feeds it through so he can distort it. That's not what I'm going to do. When I'm using musicians there's not going to be any radios. I'm just using the radio when I'm on my own.

"When I use the musicians I would be in the centre of the mandala with the grand piano as a receptor. The five musicians would have gestures and movements to do and so on. It's a subtle difference between Stockhausen and myself, but we are one Stalag different.

"There's only one place I can think of in Canada and that's looking down onto the mezzanine floor of the National Gallery (Al shows a picture of the floor's mandala). With the piano in the centre, and as I repeat, a medium. The spectacle would be for various mandalas, there would be costumes or gestures or things. Wouldn't it be great? It's awful pretty in my head. *BeBopARoonie!* I've got to play some music that's too much for words."

Al Neil moves to his piano, such as it is—as a child advances upon a favorite, well-worn toy. They both play with the same kind of immersion, the same loss of self in the greater energy of the imagination that makes one reconsider the old notion of the artist as magician.

For if it is magical for us to sit there and watch an aging pianist suddenly become ageless, like some rain forest leprechaun, whose language is musical, non-referential but purely emotive, then pause momentarily in your straight life and try to conceptualize what changes are happening to Al Neil.

If he says he's plugging in to the Creator, who's to argue?

Don Van Vliet: Know What I Mean?

Holiday Inn, Vancouver, March, 1973

BEEFHEART AT THE COMMODORE BALLROOM. Do you know what I mean? Too many tables, too long between two sets to get too drunk, too many sitters, too many decibels, too few with it, after all. The Captain (*a.k.a.* Don Van Vliet) motions stand up, people yell siddown; good vibes, bad vibes. Ace DJ Bob Ness and I sitting, standing, laughing at the crowd and wondering at the stage. Vice versa. The Band magical—tight in execution, wondrous in content. Where do such riffs come from? Do they ever go back? Can we go with them? Beefheart's *a capella* singing of *Black Snake Blues*. Hubbub. The Captain hisses snake sounds, sighs, snaps, slithers offstage. Scandal?

We meet after the gig, backstage, and an interview is set up back at the Holiday Inn. We walk. Arrive 2 am, sit down and set up. Zoot Horn Rollo and Ed Marimba (with green moustache) keep things moving along.

Finally The Captain arrives, announces he thinks Alice Cooper "failed erector set," and when asked what he means by that, the answer comes: "I think he does number paintings and tries to make a big deal out of it. Do you know what I mean?" And on that note I started this, my last interview for *The Terminal City Express*—my last gig as an underground press rock writer.

Rick McGrath: You had some difficulty on stage?

Don Van Vliet: I dug it. You mean the monitors?

McGrath: During Black Snake Blues?

Don Van Vliet: Oh, well, people were making noises and they felt guilty about making them. You see, everything's in key until you take it out of key. And some of the people who were making those noises evidently felt guilty or didn't think they were supposed to make noises and upon not thinking they weren't supposed to make noises, they went out of key, you see?

And I couldn't sing with all those outta keys. If they had just made noises like an animal makes noises, involuntarily; like a fish doesn't go around snapping his bubbles, doesn't even know he's making them. You know what I mean? When we go up there we're just combing out our hair, and we don't know we're combing our hair. We're not looking in a mirror. They were making noises, looking in a mirror, and there's a distortion.

Do you understand what I mean? I'm just off the stage, and it takes me a long time to get back to the old world. Not that you're from the old world. That's not what I'm saying. It just takes me a long time to get it together to be able to talk. Because music's different than talking, even singing. You know that.

McGrath: I can dig it. Dissonance is diss. You have a new album, Clear Spot?

Don Van Vliet: I like it. It's my favourite album of all I've done. Because the group's getting together. Now they're getting together more than when we did the album. Now I've got back Alex Sinclair, the fellow who taught Hendrix and Townshend. Hell, yes he did. We went to England and they didn't know what a slide was. Seven years ago. They didn't know what singin' was, either.

They were going like this (sings falsetto vibrato) and we were into it. They thought we were really weird, way out. One guy thought I was a drunken methadone addict at a speakeasy and the guy's name was John Lennon. The album was written in two hours in a station wagon going to a job. It was the way I felt at that time.

McGrath: Were the horns added after the fact?

Don Van Vliet: No, I wrote them out. Charts. I did them on a tape and had them transcribed by Art Tripp, who spent seven and a half years at the Manhattan School of Music.

McGrath: Do you record the music and then the lyrics?

Don Van Vliet: Unfortunately, I sing so hard I have to do that. I'd love to sing with the band, but it just won't work, because my voice leaks into their instruments. Which is what its supposed to do—but in a controlled manner—or else it doesn't come out properly on a disc, which is a drag.

McGrath: Have you ever recorded the voice first, then the instruments?

Don Van Vliet: On *Trout Mask Replica* I turned the tracks off when I sang. And on *Lick My Decals Off Baby* I played the horn with the tracks off on *Flash Gordon's Ape*. It's no problem for me to know where to come in and out. It's not even a challenge, if you want to know the truth.

McGrath: Are you still playing the horn?

Don Van Vliet: Oh, I am, I am.

McGrath: You said on Bob Ness' radio show you felt like a harp this year.

Don Van Vliet: I do, but occasionally I will pick up the horn—but it's the same as somebody picking up a rock and throwing it, making it skip across the water. It's not that important to me. Do you know what I mean? I like to sing more than I like to play the horn. They got real serious about me blowin' the horn.

McGrath: Who did?

Don Van Vliet: Well, *Downbeat*, all the jazz people. Those guys were serious, man, and when they get that serious, forget it. I'm not that serious, because getting that serious defeats the purpose of playing the horn. Can you imagine a fish that would be serious about it's bubble? It would choke to death. That's what it sounds to me a lot of singers and musicians have been doing for the last 150 years.

McGrath: What are you reading?

Don Van Vliet: The first book I ever read in my life was just recently. I got all Fs in school; of course, I only went to see the girls. I mean, what can they teach you? You want to be a different fish, you've got to get out of the school. And seeing the way the other fish were going I sure didn't want to be in there. I didn't want to murder Indians and Black people. And eat white sugar, and advocate all that ridiculous political... uhh... what is it? If you don't mind stupid people in high places, you don't mind government.

So I didn't really go to school, you see. Because I'm a painter, really, and a sculptor, so what good would it have done me to go to school? Just to have somebody move my hand the way somebody did for years, real stiff, and then tell me to look through thousands of eyes and then try to find my own at the end of it. That's bullshit.

It's good for some people, depending on what you want to do. If you want to be a filing clerk, well, there's lots of ways of being a filing clerk. You know what I mean? I read a book recently called *Sting Like A Bee* and it's one of the first things this guy's ever written, and it's written about Mohammed Ali, who's my favourite percussionist. I like him a lot. He's a nice fellow. I like his timing; I don't listen to his poetry.

McGrath: What are you: entertainer, artist, or regular fellow?

Don Van Vliet: I never think about that, to tell you the truth. But now you've got me thinking about it. I think I'm a... uhh... I don't know what I am.

I'll tell you the truth. They have these fellows who have nets, right? Butterfly nets. If I were a butterfly, I'd want a net with just the hoop to go over me. Do you know what I mean? I don't like chewing gum, it sticks you up.

McGrath: You like puns. I talked with you before you went onstage the last time you were here, and your puns were better.

Don Van Vliet: They're better before or after?

McGrath: Before you go onstage.

Don Van Vliet: The thing is, my wife told me not to pun anymore, because it was making all these people money, and she says that we should make the money. So, I'm writing books and not putting them out for publication. If I'm to eat my hat, Zappa's whole lyrics were written by me, fifteen years ago.

McGrath: Yeah, you should have written them down.

Don Van Vliet: I did. That doesn't mean anything in this business. I've got about 45,000 songs written and I have at least 150 full-length novels—whatever a full-length novel is. I've got some as big as a phone book. I get up and do 150 pages a day like you get up and do a push-up. I have to—it's my exercise. Otherwise, I get too intellectual and I don't like it—it gets too ridiculous. I find myself watching my bubbles like a crazy fish. Men do that.

Women usually aren't too intellectual. Women are right—men are the ones who have the trouble. You know what I'm saying. Possibly because of our society. Women can usually flow a lot easier than men. It does depend on the individual, but more women are not watching their footsteps. You see more men watching their footsteps. Men like to trip themselves—they get a thing out of it.

McGrath: Very cool. Speaking of flow, what's your vocal range?

Don Van Vliet: Seven and a half octaves. On a piano I go off the bass. It doesn't register where I go. It happens naturally, but people who work at it usually have two, or two and a half. I can do every note in those seven and a half octaves. I was going to do it during the show, but they got me all out of key and out of time. I was ready to do it, too. I was going to go into it, but—it just takes you being loose, really loose. Then again there's not much to be tight about.

McGrath: You do have concerns, though. I know you're concerned about whales...

Don Van Vliet: I write a lot of things about the environment. I'm really mad about what they're doing to whales, for instance. I'm not mad, I'm infuriated. Those things are brilliant and I think they're bums for doing that. I've heard their music, and it's past trigonometry, calculus, past polygraphs and beyond that.

They're smart, and it's frightening that we're killing them. I think the people who are killing them are not as smart as they are. No way are they as smart as a whale, or even a dolphin. I think their IQs are way higher than the average person's, from what I hear of their music. Have you ever read *A Whale For The Killing*? My wife read that to me. I got it in Newfoundland when I was up there.

McGrath: You played Newfoundland?

Don Van Vliet: Yeah, it was good. I liked it.

McGrath: Amazing. Most Canadians have never been there. You making good money?

Don Van Vliet: You know I'm going to make a lot of zeroes. You know that, don't you? You can tell. You heard the group tonight and you know they're really commercial. Let's face it. We're as commercial as the Rolling Stones when they first started, before they got above their belt.

These guys are still below their belt, sound-wise. And that's what makes money. We're going to be doing $300,000 worth of business in Europe. That's after taxes. There's a lot of money in this business. I've never really been hurting, you know. They say this, but I haven't. I can't stop them from saying it.

I'll survive. I've got a lot of property in Northern California, and when I get to the point I have a lot of money from this corporation—I sink it mostly into my corporation, God's Golfball—then I'm going to help—first animals, then people.

McGrath: Interesting you would choose animals over people.

Don Van Vliet: You can help animals—people are very hard to help. When The Beatles were singing *I Want To Hold Your Hand* I was singing to watch out for Strontium 90, let's put it that way. And you see how big they made it, compared to me. But I'm still going. All of *Trout Mask Replica* was about ecology.

McGrath: Is Blabber And Smoke aimed at ecology freaks?

Don Van Vliet: I think a lot of them are shucks. And I think they're doing it to identify themselves into something they thought was lame a week ago. All of a sudden they like animals. But it's more important that they help animals, rather than like them.

It's important that they like them, but why don't they help them, rather than talk about how bitchin' they are because they like them?

McGrath: Ever thought about getting actively involved?

Don Van Vliet: Well, I'm doing all I can about it. And I'm growing more and more accessible. Then I'll be able to say more. And the people I think are involved directly will be able to do it, and I don't think it's important for me to go and wave a banner in the middle of Washington or something. But I hope it helps. Usually they take whatever trend at the time there is, and they put the thing away. Then they go to the next thing.

McGrath: What are your feelings on dope?

Don Van Vliet: Like Garcia, I don't dig anybody who tells little kids to take poison when they listen to their music. What the hell has that got to do with music? Nothing I've even thought of. Not only acid, but worse than that all the way—AMA drugs and all that. Go to the drug store, choose your favourite narcotic. All that crap—you know what I mean?

Bob Dylan & The Band

Live at The Seattle Center Coliseum, Seattle, February 9, 1974.
Rick McGrath Photos

ShaNaNa

Live at The University of British Columbia Gynasium, November 7, 1974.
Rick McGrath Photos

Van Morrison & The Street Band

Live at the University of British Columbia Auditorium, February 17, 1974.
Tracey Hearst Photos

LARRY CORYELL

Live at The Egress, Vancouver, 1974.
Tracey Hearst Photos

Joan Baez

Live in Vancouver, 1974.
Rick McGrath Photos

Tim Buckley

Live at The Egress, Vancouver, 1974.
Tracey Hearst Photos

THE TUBES

Live at The Gardens Auditorium, 1976.
Rick McGrath Photos

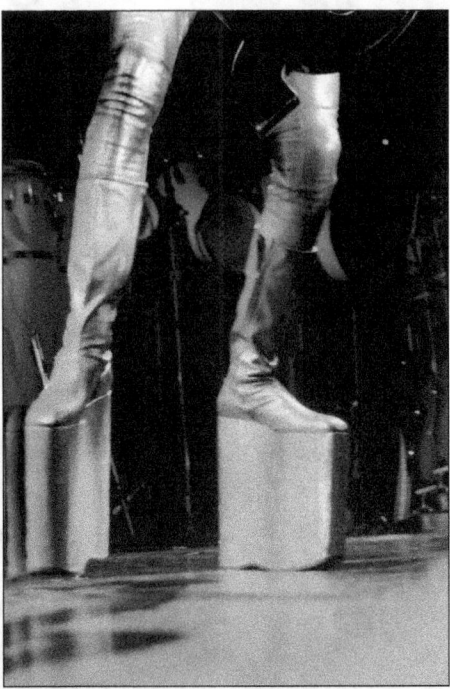

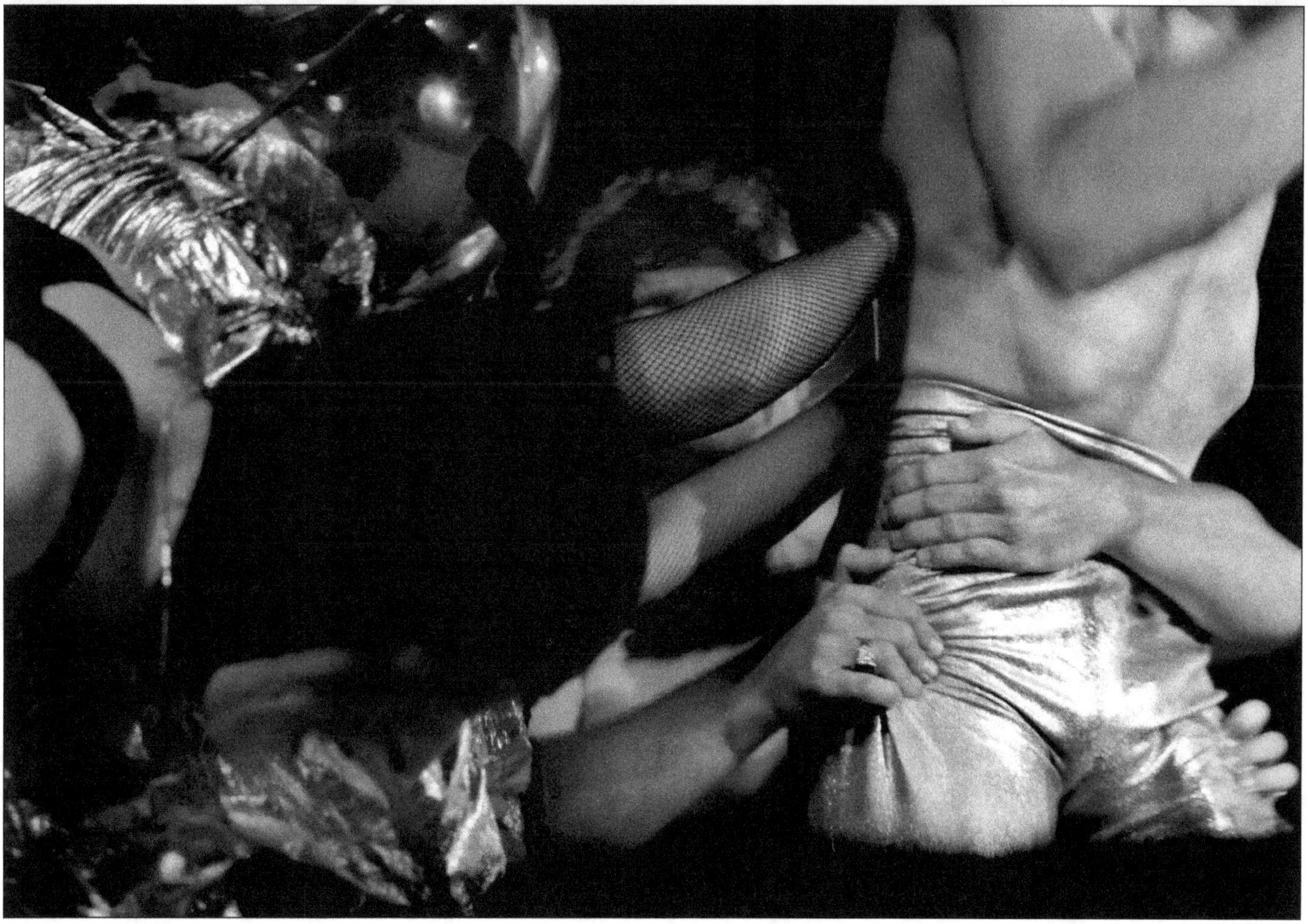

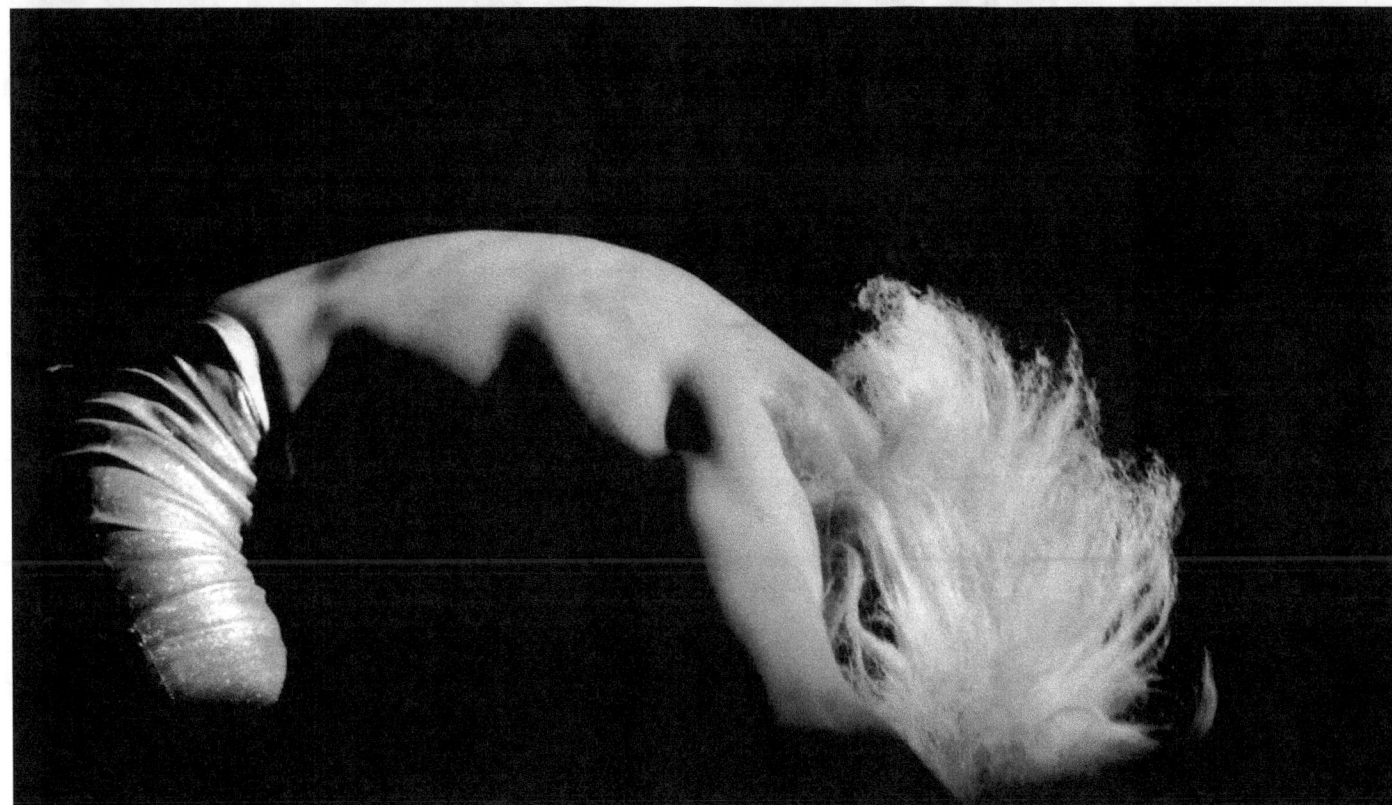

John Fahey

Rick McGrath Photos

TOM RAPP & PEARLS BEFORE SWINE

The Georgia Straight, January 6, 1971

HERE'S A PIECE OF CULT PIE. Does anyone remember psychedelic troubadour Tom Rapp and his rather elitist-sounding band, Pearls Before Swine? I always thought the group's name made flashing the front of these albums at the checkout a problematic decision. But just how hip was this stuff? Hip. And who is he? Oh, yeah: Tom Rapp is an imaginative folkie from North Dakota who popped into the minor leagues in 1967 with the trendily-monickered *One Nation Underground* album—certainly appealing to an underground newspaper—that featured the Arlo Guthrie-inspired *Miss Morse*, which used the selfsame code to spell out a word not usually heard on FM radio, to wit:

Oh Dear, Miss Morse, I want you,
Oh yes, I do, I want you.
This may strike you odd-i-ly
But I want you bodily

Don't blame me dear, blame McLuhan
His media were your ruin

Chorus:
Dit Dit Dah Dit
Dit Dit Dah
Dah Dit Dah Dit
Dah Dit Dah

Four letters... *hmmm*. But yes, clever. Anyway, to explain this piece—Rapp's fourth Warner album, *Beautiful Lies You Could Live In*, had just been released and the promo man brought me all four of them, which I played mostly out of curiosity (there are many English literature references) and was rewarded with an amazing trip. Some of Tom's albums are now CDs and available, and Tom himself, after retiring from music to become a civil rights lawyer, released his final album, *A Journal of the Plague Year*, in 1999. This is my 1971 article:

PART I

Imagine you're a member of a rock band. You're trying to make it.

Now, imagine a combination of the Everglades and the corner of the biggest downtown intersection in the city of Your Choice. That's where you are when you start out. The aim of the game is to get out of the swamp and light the city on fire.

If you get rich, just consider it a replacement of greenery. If you don't get out, don't despair—the hole is bottomless and everyone's intentions are biodegradable.

PART II

Imagine you're a member of a rock band. You don't care if you make it. Imagine you're a singer/songwriter. You start out in the swamp and you dig it. Sure, you may have bumped shoulders with Bob Dylan once, or had a couple of quiet chats with Leonard Cohen, or maybe read a little too much Kurt Vonnegut, but basically you're still the same.

You're doing what you want to do—and you're not listening to you or me. You're not rich, but you're happy.

PART III

In 1967 the music was still blowing chunks in the wind in the eastern half of the United States. Psychedelia was blooming, but the flowers were children on the west coast. It seemed like everybody and everything was involved in a last gasping drag on mystic Romanticism: *See Me, Hear Me, Touch Me*, because *I Sense, Therefore I Am*. East Coast rock was reaching almost to the pre-Dylan low, but something was definitely on the move. And the move moved with a group called Pearls Before Swine.

Pearls Before Swine first surfaced out of the swamps with the aid of a rather unique recording outfit called ESP Records. They managed to make almost everything sound like a cassette recording in someone's basement, but of all the little recording companies, it perhaps had the most guts and the most foresight. Anyway, ESP recorded Pearls Before Swine, and in the winter of 1968 their first album, *One Nation Underground*, was released.

The initial reaction, strangely enough, concerned the lyrics: a collection of Paul Simon's nightmares? Leonard Cohen on a bummer? The man responsible for the songs, and, in fact, the man responsible for PBS, turned out to be a skinny little dude from North Dakota called Thomas Rapp.

Tom Rapp started out doing the things that make us think of "artists" from an early age. He got his start in life in Lawrence Welk's hometown of Bottineau, North Dakota.

By the time he was six he had begun to play the ukulele and had moved to Pine Island and then to Northfield, Minn. The first song came at seven, and Tom found himself performing in talent shows. There was a story circulating that Tom and Bob Zimmerman both entered the same contest: Tom came in second; Bob sixth.

Just goes to show you never can tell—guitar lessons came at nine, Pennsylvania at ten and by the time he was twelve, Tom had given up on the whole pop music trip. In lieu of the locally produced American Bandstand, Tom turned his rather precocious hand to writing stories, painting and reading science fiction.

Then things got a little intellectual: president of his high school Latin club, twice second place winner at a local college science fair and an award for "excellence in the study of current events."

The boy was a goody two-shoes.

In 1965, Tom graduated from high school and wrote his second song, reputedly inspired by Walter Cronkite's TV news sidekick, Eric Sevareid.

Between the time Tom graduated and the release of his first album in May 1967, he worked for eighteen straight months at a McDonald's hamburger joint, met a few musicians, and made a home tape. ESP dug it.

Tom then stuck around long enough to drop out of junior college and then Florida State. In a rare personal appearance Tom & The Pearls graced Anderson Theatre, New York. It was February, 1968. The *New York Times* pop critic said, "Pearls, indeed." The last ESP disc, entitled *Balaklava*, also appeared in 1968, and then the first of their four Reprise discs, *These Things Too*, happened in 1969.

PART IV

To talk about Pearls' music is to talk about Tom Rapp's music. For Rapp is the mastermind behind the concept: what he doesn't write, he borrows, and what he borrows he still turns to his own use. His music may be understood in part by the artists who have influenced his way of looking at the world. The first Reprise album, *These Things Too* (RS 6364), starts out with a song called *Footnote* that sort of sets the whole tone of Rapp's philosophy and intellectual intent. The words are by W.H. Auden:

> perfection of a kind was what he was after
> the poetry he invented was easy to understand
> he knew human folly like the back of his hand
> he had an interest in armies and fleets
> when he laughed respectable senators
> laughed at his feet
> but when he cried the little children died in the streets

Most of Rapp's own poetry follows the same ironic progression from dry, sarcastic wit to pathos. There is a clear eye and almost Dylan-like quality to the opening of another song on this disc, called *If You Don't Want To (I Don't Mind)*:

>   was a time
>   lost on mobius street
>   with no where to go
>   well the times were so low

The disc also contains a very fine rendition of Dylan's *I Shall Be Released* (even before it became popular), a quaint little French love song composed for his wife, Elizabeth (her fine voice is heard on all four albums), and a rather folkish instrumental number.

The overriding mood of these first albums is one of almost idealized pessimism, expressed in the *The Wizard of Is* song:

>   everything you see around you
>   will roll away on wheels of tomorrow
>   down misty willow rivers of because
>   into the land of was

Musically, this album also marked the beginnings of one of the best unions to come about in rock: Rapp and the studio musician. Tom seems to always get the best and inspire the best from them. *These Things Too* boasts the talents of Bill Salter on bass, Grady Tate on drums, Richard Greene on incredible electric violin, Eric Weisberg, Bill Eaton, and quite a few more.

The harmonies do have a distinctive old folkie quality about them, sure, but the arrangements are tidy little things that accentuate Rapp's slightly jazzy, Jesse Colin Young kind of vocalizing. The second Reprise disc, *The Use Of Ashes* (RS 6405), takes *These Things Too* and places them under a glass for closer scrutiny. There is still an emphasis on death, war and human misunderstandings, but the razor edge that cuts the images is slightly more incisive this time around.

People like Charlie McCoy, Kenny Buttry & David Briggs (those Nashville cats) round out the musical end, but it still remains Rapp's lyrics and incredible voice that give the lasting impression:

>   the jeweler has a shop on the corner of the boulevard
>   in the night, in small spectacles, he polishes old coins
>   he uses spit and cloth and ashes
>   he makes them shine with ashes
>   he knows the use of ashes
>   he worships god with ashes

The third album, *City Of Gold* (Reprise 6442) finds Rapp taking a slightly different look at his surroundings. The first cut is, well, what would you call Shakespeare's Sonnet #65...

>   Since brass nor stone nor earth, nor boundless sea,
>   But sad mortality o'er sways their power,
>   How with this rage shall beauty hold a plea,
>   Whose action is no stronger than a flower?

…when warbled through plugged nasal cavities to a super C&W harmony. Shakespeare was pondering the strange power of physical beauty, and Rapp adds his own thoughts to the ancient problem: "The lives and deaths of promises always rise and link together and surround us: so it comes down to whether we are, brick by brick, building a city or tearing it down." The album is an exploration of that statement—an exploration of it within the framework of the so-called youth culture.

PART V

And now we have the latest PBS offering: *Beautiful Lies You Could Live In* (Reprise 6467). The front cover shows J.E. Millias' painting of *Ophelia*, love mad, clutching her flowers, her dress billowing around her in the waters of the moat, just before it becomes water-soaked and drags her to death.

Again the preoccupation with a Shakespearean theme, again the irony of the title. The optimism of the last record (and there was damn little to start with) is again pushed backwards, and Rapp forces us into melancholy with songs like Cohen's *Bird on a Wire*, an A.E. Houseman poem, *Epitaph on an Army of Mercenaries*, and a Lennonish *Everybody's Got Pain*.

Again the music is very strong, with Billy Mundi, Stu Scharf, Amos Garrett, Herb Lovell, Gerry Jermott, etc., helping Tom out.

But it is not, certainly, this preoccupation with deathly or morbid or pessimistic themes that makes Tom Rapp interesting. Rapp is important because he has a fine mind, a well developed musical talent, and a clean, sure, distinct way of expressing himself.

In the muddle of semi-profound and pretentious lyrics that send today's record-buying masses into fits of poetic banality (you know who they are) Rapp and his rather prophetic Pearls may be a throw in the right direction.

Rolling Stones: Shelter Needed

Toronto, 2001

Ooh, a storm is threatening my very life today
If I don't get some shelter, oh yeah I'm gonna fade away
War, children, it's just a shot away, it's just a shot away
War, children, it's just a shot away, it's just a shot away

Shelter Given.

YOU DON'T FORGET the first time you experience *Gimme Shelter*. I had tickets for the film's opening matinee in Vancouver, shown on December 6, 1970, and when I blinked into the sunlight after the movie I was suddenly being interviewed by a local TV station. I don't remember any of what transpired—probably an example of selective memory—but I hope I said then what I said in 2001 when I reviewed this film for the website *Culture Court*: *Gimme Shelter* is a deft and subtle film that's more movie than documentary, a chilling exercise in voyeurism that allows the audience to ironically participate in a pocket of violence which came to symbolize the end of the so-called counter culture phenomenon of the late 1960s.

Unlike *Cocksucker Blues*, the suppressed film of the Stones' notorious 1972 North American tour, *Gimme Shelter* reeks of professional technique, clever ideas, and lots of cash.

You'll not see many opening scenes like the in-your-face start to *Gimme Shelter*. We begin with The Stones doing a bit of Beatles-like dressup spoofery on a road, which then cuts to Madison Square Garden for a hopped-up rendition of *Jumpin Jack Flash*, which segues into Charlotte Zwerin's editing suite in London, where a bemused Mick Jagger is watching himself on an editing screen.

Whoa. From fantasy to acting to reality in three quantum leaps. Now jump to Charlie Watts listening to Hell's Angels leader Sonny Barger make excuses for the Angels' activities.

"I ain't no cop," he snarls. "They were messing with our bikes." Now jump to Jagger, looking very nervous as Barger says Jagger may be fingering the Angels as the perpetrators, but that's not the way he sees it. It's completely riveting, and you're hooked on all the themes right off the bat. Or pool cue.

Director/Film Editor Charlotte Zwerin has to be given credit for the film's fascinating structure. In a flash of genius she asked members of The Stones to drop round her editing suite and check out the raw footage. They agreed, and cameras were set up to catch their reactions.

Suddenly the film morphs from a documentary into something else, something doubly voyeuristic. This double removal from the action means the film takes on a timeless feeling, as the present in the film is forever locked to those moments when The Stones watch the rough cuts and then watch The Stones watch The Stones watching the rough cuts—you get the idea.

So the "documentary", which reveals the story in a narrative timeframe is now fragmented into flashbacks. This startling new structure means *Gimme Shelter* not a true documentary, but not really fiction, either. What we witness is a powerful new combination of reality and fiction, told through action and reaction.

This structure, this self-referential mirror, is also the perfect way (perhaps the only way) for The Stones to deflect charges that they were responsible for the Altamont concert, which not only filled the void with bad vibes but which wiped out all the good vibes of Woodstock, which I was surprised to remember was a mere four months earlier.

Ahh, the power of symbolism. Having Barger accuse Jagger right off the top was no doubt a calculated risk on Sir Mick's part, but it works, and any ideas you might have about the Angels being non-instigators is completely shattered by the end of the concert. But The Stones don't emerge unscathed, either. It's freaky to watch Jagger watching himself at a news conference. "That's bullshit," he remarks to the onscreen Jagger, who has tried to be charming and glib with a female reporter.

Mick has nothing to say next, however, as he watches himself tell the media about this free concert, a concert that will show the world how a large group of people can get together and behave like the idealized hippy.

The Irony Fairly Oozes.

Cut to a camera-loving Melvin Belli, relishing the fact he can phone up important people and speak on behalf of "The Rolling Stones," and you already start to see why this ill-conceived concert was just about to slide into the toaster.

Not Just Another Snuff Movie.

It's odd, but even exhaustive research of this movie reveals little of its status as a snuff film. Hey, we actually get to see the unfortunate Meredith Hunter being stabbed, zoomed right up close and in slow motion, and unlike the visually degraded Zapruder film, this is shot in glorious 16mm colour by a professional cameraman. And it's real.

A Celebration of Technique.

You can't watch this movie and not be impressed by the way it comes together. All the shots are great, and Zwerin's editing is unbelievably tight. The film's unusual structure gives her mind-wrenching leeway in terms of cuts, because she can always segue to the present for a comment or reaction, and escape the chronological boundaries of the basic storyline. One might expect this bouncing back and forth to become a tad tedious after awhile, but to Zwerin's credit most are natural and flowing. A few are incredible.

This "time bounce" structure also takes advantage of the lack of filmed material Zwerin had to work with. Essentially, there are lots of shots of Altamont, a bit shot in Belli's office, a bit shot in a hotel room, the Muscle Shoals bit and the MSG concert. There may also be footage from a west coast concert—nothing is identified. Zwerin skillfully moves to each from her home base at the editing table, and magically seems to stretch the beginning to balance off the wildly overshot Altamont sequence (for which the Maysles used 22 cameramen, including a young George Lucas, and 14 Nagra-toting soundmen).

Extra Goodies Abound.

Criterion wildly overcharges for their so-called arty flicks, and *Gimme Shelter* is no exception. You do, however, receive a fair number of extra goodies:

- Never-before-seen performances of the Rolling Stones at Madison Square Garden in 1969, including *Little Queenie*, *Oh Carol* and *Prodigal Sun*, plus backstage outtakes
- Audio commentary by directors Albert Maysles and Charlotte Zwerin, and collaborator Stanley Goldstein
- A 44-page booklet (this is fascinating—it contains all the tech specs, plus six essays on the Altamont concert, including one from the always-acrimonius Angel Sonny Barger—he still blames the "sissy, marble-mouthed prima donna" Stones for everything)
- Altamont stills gallery, featuring the work of photographers Bill Owens and Beth Sunflower
- Originals and re-releases of theatrical trailers, plus trailers for Maysles Films' classics *Grey Gardens* and *Salesman*
- Excerpts from KSAN radio's Altamont wrap-up, recorded December 7, 1969, with new introductions by then-DJ Stefan Ponek
- Restoration demonstration
- Filmographies for Maysles Films and Charlotte Zwerin
- English subtitles

Looking into a Heavy Space.

There is no doubt *Gimme Shelter* is a masterpiece. The overwhelming wrong-way reality of it all reaches out to tell its story in ways the Ancient Mariner never dreamed of.

The story: compelling.

The acting: well, if you think a 150-pound Mick Jagger, dressed in a ludicrous outfit and quickly losing control of the onstage situation while being stared at by uncomprehending, armed, doped-up Angels is acting, then the acting is great.

The death of the Age of Aquarius: you still listen to Donovan? The question of hubris: Jagger is damned. The reality of violence: it happens a lot faster than you think. The marketing of rock stars: the boys come across as hard-working and straight. Wow. A clue. There's a lot of heavy shit going on in these 91 minutes, and what emerges is a lot deeper than just a rock'n'roll movie with a bad ending.

In many ways, this film created the myth of Altamont—just as the music and the movie shaped the myth of Woodstock into a trippy Nirvana/Eden for people too wasted to help themselves. With great background music. *Gimme Shelter* creates the myth of Jagger as The Devil, and destroys it by showing Mick wearing the emperor's clothes. It's that audacious irony that separates *Gimme Shelter* from all other rock tour flicks. Personally, I could care less about the film's subplot of apportioning blame. It's ancient history.

Today, the Hell's Angels don't guard rock concerts, they sell the drugs consumed at rock concerts. And what kind of a space were we in to think that collecting 300,000 plus people in one place to listen to rock stars—and do it without fighting!—was something that was good and could set our generation apart. Were we crazy? Must have been stoned, for sure. And tribal.

Today, *Gimme Shelter* doesn't have the emotional baggage that made it devilishly red hot in the 1970s. And that's probably a good thing, because today you can watch it and appreciate it for what it really is: a chance, dramatic happenstance, brilliantly captured on film and even more brilliantly edited into a pandora's box of a movie.

Rolling Stones: Cocksucker Blues

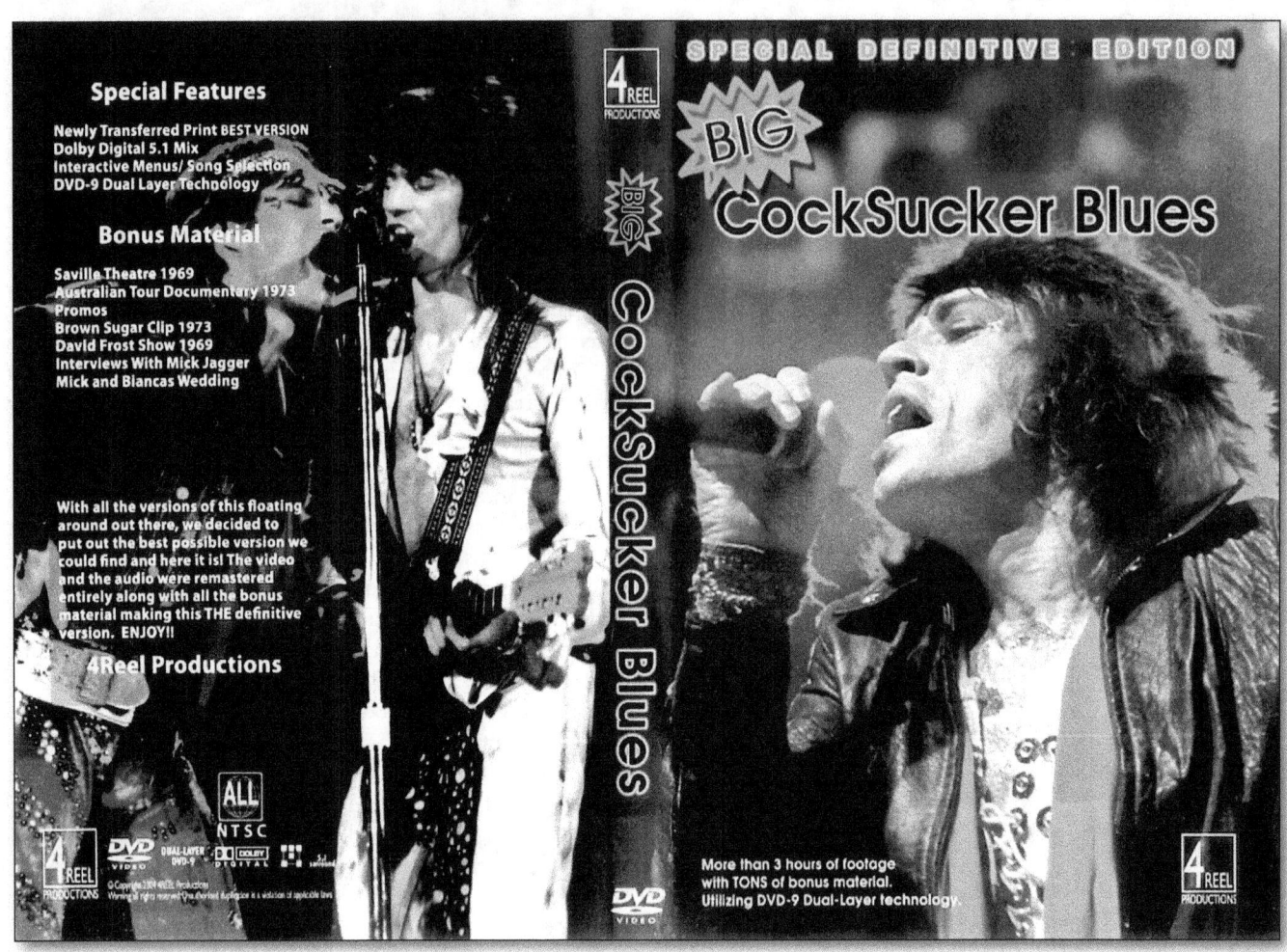

Toronto, July, 2001

OF ALL THE CRAZY TOURS The Rolling Stones have made across North America, the 1972 Stones Touring Party (STP) is still remembered as the most outrageous, most provocative, most inventive musical outing the fab five from London ever performed.

I was fortunate enough to see this juicy juggernaut when it made its stop in Vancouver on Saturday, June 3rd, 1972. Vancouver was chosen as the first gig of this two-month tour, and wouldn't you know it?—while the kick-off concert amused and confused the Stoners inside the building, the party outside had a setlist that rocked to a riot when 2,000 fans tried to crash the Pacific Coliseum and 31 Vancouver cops were injured in the subsequent melee. I reviewed the concert in the June 7, 1972 edition of *The Grape*, noting: "The Stones' playing on a few songs, certainly the new ones from *Exile on Main Street*, was a bit sloppy. But when one takes into consideration this was the first gig of the tour, the odd missed beat or note was understandable.

What was more important was the fact they all seemed to be having fun, despite the rather chintzy elements of their over-the-top stage show. Jagger, dressed all in white, was certainly more angelic than sinister, and as he crawled around the huge stage flailing a biker's belt during *Midnight Rambler* the total effect was one of self-parody rather than an echo of the bikers at Altamont a mere 18 months earlier."

As STP expert Harold Colsen reports: "The fabled summer 1972 tour through the U.S. and Canada is revered by Stones fans worldwide as arguably the band's greatest ever, and it remains enshrined in the annals of rock lore and popular imagination as the masterpiece speedball of indoor triumph, outdoor maelstrom, and backstage debauch. In powerful testament to this enduring sway, vast quantities of audio recordings, books, magazines, photographs, films, videos, and other memorabilia have since issued through licit and sub-licit channels to keep the coveted sights and sounds of the Stones Touring Party alive, rolling, and fresh to this very day." *Cocksucker Blues* is one of those enduring sub-licit channels which not only celebrates the fore, middle and background of this tour, but which also presents itself as one of the very best rock tour movies ever made, and never seen.

This review was written in 2001 for the website *Culture Court* after I was able to find myself a rare bootleg DVD of Robert Frank's amazing documentary of the tour.

Have You Heard About The... It's Not One Of Those.

Here's the scene: The Stones have not visited the US since the 1969 disaster of Altamont—also immortalized by the Brothers Maysles in the tour/performance flick *Gimme Shelter*—and the group is riding high and hard on the success of their definitive album, *Exile On Main Street*. Myth-mad Mick, despite the surprisingly frank shots of *Gimme Shelter*, decides to do the film thing one more time and enlists the talent of famous photog/filmmaker Robert Frank (he shot the pix on the *Exile* album cover as well as a brutal documentary on madness, called *Me and My Brother*).

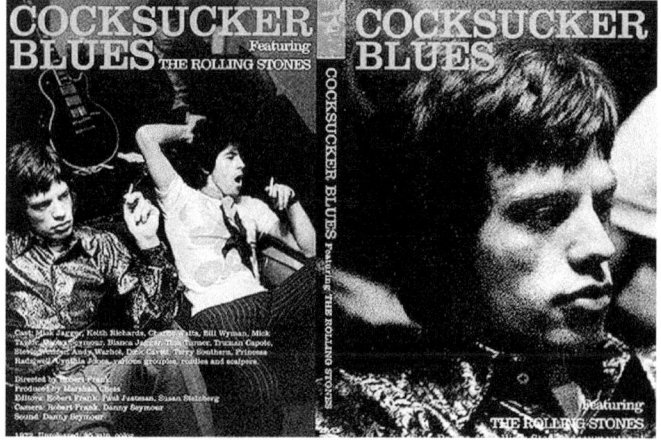

Cast: Mick Jagger, Keith Richards, Charlie Watts, Bill Wyman, Mick Taylor, Danny Seymour, Bianca Jagger, Tina Turner, Stevie Wonder, Andy Warhol, Dick Cavett, Princess Radziwell, Terry Southern, Cynthia Jones, Truman Capote, various groupies, roadies and scalpers.

Director: Robert Frank

Producer: Marshall Chess

Editors: Robert Frank, Paul Justman, Susan Steinberg

Camera: Robert Frank, Danny Seymour

Sound: Danny Seymour

In comes producer Marshall Chess, who, early in the movie, gives the plotline: Mick has already written a song called *Cocksucker Blues*, about a gay hooker in London, to fulfill the group's contractual obligations to Decca records, which was run at the time by an old fart named Sir Edward Lewis. Apparently, during a meeting Mick gets up and plays a demo of the song to the uptight geezer—the lyrics of which are:

Well, I'm a lonesome schoolboy
and I just came into town
Yeah, I'm a lonesome schoolboy
and I just came into town
Well, I heard so much about London
I decided to check it out

Well, I wait in Leicester Square
with a come-hither look in my eye
Yeah, I'm leaning on Nelson's Column
but all I do is talk to the lime

Chorus:
Oh where can I get my cock sucked?
Where can I get my ass fucked?
I may have no money,
but I know where to put it every time

Well, I asked a young policeman
if he'd only lock me up for the night
Well, I've had pigs in the farmyard,
some of them, some of them, they're alright?
Well, he fucked me with his truncheon
and his helmet was way too tight

Repeat Chorus

Needless to say, this winsome ditty had the desired effect, and the song was never released. Chess goes on to say some cat in New York was organizing a benefit for London's *Oz Magazine*, which was being hassled by the government in an obscenity trial, and the idea came up to do a porno album, with rock stars contributing "adult" material to raise dough for the underground magazine.

Cocksucker Blues was one song, and there were others, like Dr John (The Night Tripper)'s *You Can Never Eat Too Much Pussy*. Then the idea expanded from an album to a film—which this isn't. Shot cinema verité, docu-rocku style, *Cocksucker Blues* is a pinball machine of images—soft, warm, harsh, exploitative, funny, sad, boring, stupid and smart, jammed with images of excessive hard drug taking, nodding-off Stones, roadies fucking groupies, backstage parties, naked women, heroin shoot-ups, and, yes, some great concert footage.

The film is, however, so over the top that when it was finished The Stones banned its release and obtained a court injunction against its distribution. Cinematographer Frank finally got the rights to screen the flick once a year, but at the time of writing one could only obtain this movie on video in bootleg form.

I'm Bored. How About Some Sex & Drugs?

Filmmaker Jim Jarmusch, commenting on *Cocksucker Blues*, called it "definitely one of the best movies about rock and roll I've ever seen. It makes you think being a rock and roll star is one of the last things you'd ever want to do." Amen to that.

One has the feeling these guys are soldiers, waiting for the next battle, the next opportunity to feel alive. In the meantime, there's the tedium, confusion, boredom, and good old angst & ennui of being locked into a big money, big stadium, big everything rock tour.

Director Frank unblinkingly reveals these patterns of unrest behind The Stone's bulletproof window of fame, showing us the ever-present drugs and groupies, Keith Richards' addiction to heroin, Mick Jagger's problems with the high-maintenance Bianca (who looks like Sade at a Nirvana concert) and, most interestingly, just how adroit the Glimmer Twins are at concocting and manipulating their outlaw reputations.

One of the sadder themes Frank also films is the degeneration of his friend and co-cameraman Danny Seymour, who finally succumbs to the temptations of drugs and sex around him. While not downplayed, Frank underscores the concert performances with his fascination of the backstage world, and allows the mundane sounds of the tour to set the film's themes and feel: raw and inconsequential conversations; Bianca's tiny music box; a bluesy, poignant piano theme; yammering local disc jockeys; and the nervous practice of antsy musicians just prior to going onstage.

Some Great Music. But Not Much Of It.

For a 90-minute flick, only about 15 are concert shots. We watch the boys perform the opening song for pretty well every night of the tour, *Brown Sugar*, as well as *Midnight Rambler, Everything Is All Right* (with Stevie Wonder), *I Need A Love*, and *Street Fighting Man*. *Midnight Rambler* is notable for Mick's haunting harp opening, and the band, blitzed as they are, still play very well, with Keith laying down his usual heavy chops against Mick Taylor's intelligent fills.

Mostly Classic Self-Indulgent Stuff.

No doubt shocking when shot, but now mostly clichés, given the excesses of bands which followed—Led Zeppelin being first and foremost—*Cocksucker Blues* reads like a litany of rock high priest thou shalt's:

- watch everybody snort coke & shoot heroin
- marvel at Bobby Keyes and Keith Richard as they toss a TV off their hotel balcony (first they check to see no one's below)
- thrill as Dick Cavett asks Bill Wyman, "what's running through your nervous system right now?"
- smirk as Wyman doesn't answer
- leer as Mick Jagger rubs his dink through his pants, then undoes them and gets his hand in for a better feel
- gasp as a girl trying to get into the concert complains her baby was taken from her because she's always on acid
- chuckle as a totally stoned Keith tries to order room service for some strawberries, blueberries and "three apples"
- laugh to discover a scalper is charging $10 for a $3.50 ticket
- guffaw as Mick turns to the camera after a brief meeting with Tina Turner and says "I wouldn't mind..."
- look at your watch as the boys play some very drunken poker—see Keith win
- ooh as Charlie Watts makes a very difficult pool shot in a southern diner
- moan as a naked groupie rolls on a bed, legs spread, fingering herself
- make notes as Keith tells Mick it's best to snort coke through a rolled up dollar bill
- look at your watch again as the tour crew packs the group's suitcases and cleans out their hotel rooms
- wonder in amazement as Bianca sits sullenly, smoking a cigarette and playing a little music box over and over.

The Picture Quality Sucks As Much As The Groupies.

OK, we're talking bootleg copies of the movie here. Gawd knows how many times this video has been copied before falling into my quivering hands. It's not pristine 35mm, that's for sure. On the other hand, the film itself is so zany that the highly degraded picture quality (the sound has remained pretty good) can actually add to the ethereal nature of this strange trip. My copy shows massive colour shifts to mostly blue, and the definition between colours has degenerated to almost a posterized effect. In some shots you can't really tell who the people are anymore—but does it matter? This ain't Spielberg, this is hardcore rock'n'roll, and it still has the backbeat, so you really can't lose it. I think this is the greatest rock movie ever made—probably that ever will be made, combining a talented, artistic filmmaker with the World's Greatest Rock 'n' Roll Band at the height of their glory on their craziest tour. Doesn't get much better than that.

The Prisoner: Released

Toronto, November 22, 2001

I HAVE TO TELL YOU, it was with substantial glee and dreaded anticipation that I settled down to review *The Prisoner* for the website *Culture Court,* thanks to A&E's DVD box set of all 17 episodes of this more-than-enigmatic 1960s britspy classic.

Substantial glee because I remember watching *The Prisoner* when it was first shown on CBS in 1968—I was part of a weekly gathering of university students who were vastly amused by the *anti-establishment* plots— which set up endless philosophical discussions over the "meaning" of each episode.

Not a pretty picture, granted.

I also say with dreaded anticipation because Time is a forgetful mistress, and those nostalgic memories from my carefree past might have coloured my impressions of just how great this series actually was, or wasn't. And, although it has probably been rebroadcast sporadically over the intervening years, *The Prisoner* hasn't proved to be a series which has attained any kind of popularity until the late 1990s, which is no doubt the reason behind A&E's somewhat daring decision to release the set.

For that, we can do doubt thank the obsessive nitpicking of cult *Prisoner* aficionados, who have kept the flame burning around Patrick McGoohan's eccentric vision, lighting the way for more recent generations to enjoy the socio-philosophical machinations of Number 6 and his relentlessly imaginative captors.

One thing time has taught me, however, is that to fully understand *The Prisoner* one has to go even further back than the series itself.

All the way back to 1965, and the classic spy series, *Danger Man*. Patrick McGoohan was *Danger Man*, and even though he was reputed to be the highest-paid TV actor in the UK at the time, he was also bored, bored, bored with playing the clever and dangerous John Drake, an international spy who possessed all the qualities of his cinematic rival, James Bond, except for Jimmy's tireless seduction of gorgeous women.

Danger Man/Secret Agent was a stupendous hit in the early-to-mid-1960s, making a fortune for Sir Lew Grade of ITC, elevating McGoohan to superstar status, and even making dough for singer Johnny Rivers, who cashed in on the craze with the hit song, *Secret Agent Man* in 1965. If this already seems a tad over the top, remember this was the mid-1960s, and the *symbol du jour* in those days was the ever-resourceful spy, saving the West from a plethora of bad guys, from serious to zany. Like the western genre before it, spy shows were everywhere, from James Bond and the James Coburn Flint movies on the big screen, to TV series like *The Avengers, I Spy, The Man From U.N.C.L.E., Get Smart*, and on and on. And then the unthinkable happens. McGoohan, at the peak of his powers, decides he's had enough of playing John Drake, and simply resigns from the show. He has an idea for something new, something he calls *The Prisoner*, about a spy trapped in a prison for spies.

McGoohan draws together the creative nucleus of the show, starting with producer/director David Tomblin, with whom he has already created Everyman Films, as well as story editor George Markstein and art director Jack Shampan. These people were available because they all worked on the *Danger Man* series, and were out of jobs, thanks to McGoohan's decision to retire. They get together, rough up the concept, and McGoohan takes the idea to Lew Grade. Lew buys into the idea based on a concept outline, and gives McGoohan a princely budget of £75,000 an episode (making *The Prisoner* the most expensive show of its era).

McGoohan's original plans call for seven one-hour episodes, but Sir Lew needs more to sell the show internationally. He wants 26 shows; McGoohan agrees. It's now 1966, and Sir Lew wants the show on air in a year, so there's very little time to bring all together —resulting in a production crunch which will have ramifications later on in the series.

Here's how McGoohan himself describes this episode to writer/TV host Warner Troyer in March 1977. This famous interview was done on behalf of the Ontario Educational Communications Authority, and was broadcast on TVOntario, a Canadian public television network which had shown *The Prisoner* series along with commentaries from Troyer between October 1976 and February 1977.

According to McGoohan, "I'd made 54 of those (*Danger Man/Secret Agent*) and I thought that was an adequate amount. So I went to the gentleman, Lew Grade, who was the financier, and said that I'd like to cease making *Secret Agent* and do something else. So he didn't like that idea. He'd prefer that I'd gone on forever doing it. But anyway, I said I was going to quit. So he said, 'What's the idea?' This is on the telephone initially, so I met him on a Saturday morning at 7 o'clock. That was always the time we had our discussions, and he said 'All right, what's the idea?' and I had a whole format prepared of this *Prisoner* thing which initially came to me on one of the locations on *Secret Agent* when we went to this place called Portmeirion, where a great deal of it was shot, and I thought it was an extraordinary place, architecturally and atmosphere-wise, and should be used for something and that was two years before the concept came to me.

So I prepared it and went in to see Lew Grade. I had photographs of the Village or whatever and a format and he said, 'I don't want to read the format,' because he says he doesn't read formats, he says he can't read apart from accounts, and he sort of said, 'Well, what's it about? Tell me.' So I talked for ten minutes and he stopped me and said, 'I don't understand one word you're talking about, but how much is it going to be?

So I had a budget with me, oddly enough, and I told him how much and he says, 'When can you start?' I said Monday, on scripts. And he says, 'The money will be in your company's account on Monday morning.' Which it was, and that's how we started. Behind it, of course, was a certain impatience with the numerology of society and the way we're being made into ciphers, so there was something else behind it."

Warning: this is McGoohan's version of what transpired. Like everything else about this show, even its genesis is controversial. According to Story Editor George Markstein, who left the show after the first year, ostensibly after a falling-out with McGoohan over the size of their egos, the whole concept of *The Prisoner* was his. In a rare interview before his death in the early 1990s, Markstein says: "They hoped he'd (McGoohan) go on doing a series and so I sat down at the typewriter one day— you know, any port in a storm—and typed a couple of pages. They were about a secret agent—and after all Drake had been a secret agent—who suddenly quits without any apparent reason, as McGoohan had quit without any apparent reason, and who is put away!

"I had been doing some research into the Special Operations Executive and I had come across a curious establishment that existed in Scotland during the War into which they put recalcitrant agents—and who was more recalcitrant than McGoohan!—I thought it was an excellent idea to play around with. One of the things I didn't know was what to call it, so I ended up calling it *The Prisoner*. Simple! The man was a prisoner—call it, *The Prisoner*.

"And McGoohan went for it. He was very curious about the historical, or shall we say the factual side of it. For instance, could a secret agent disappear—you know, how could someone disappear in our society and be put away somewhere? And so I waffled on about "D" notices, how the authorities can ask the news media not to reveal something, as indeed happens in our time. He was very interested, he'd never heard of "D" notices in his life and that convinced him that this fantasy horror story had—as it does in fact have—a certain foundation in fact."

Pretty cool stuff. But now it's time to get reacquainted with Number 6 and the rest of the imaginary numbers that populate *The Prisoner*. Now, decades after the show was first aired, I could mull over its mysteries anew. Mysteries? Perhaps. Or simply an intellectual baubles, brightly reflecting ideologies without a true thematic construct? It was time to find out.

No Man Is Just A Number.

The entire concept for the show is explained in the mini-play that begins each episode. Dark clouds fill the sky. Lightning flashes. Thunder rumbles. There's the sound of a jet. A long shot of a runway. Then, as the harpsichord-based theme music pulses, a Lotus Seven (KAR 120C) flashes towards us down a freeway, revealing a grim-faced man.

Cut to London streets. Cut to an underground parking lot. A man strides darkly down a corridor, dramatically throws open double doors, pounds on a balding bureaucrat's desk (played by none other than the series story editor, George Markstein), then throws down a letter of resignation and stomps out.

A machine puts Xs all over his photograph, and another machine drops his ID card into a filing cabinet marked *Resigned*. The man returns home, unaware of a following car. He grabs

his passport, starts packing some bags, and is then overcome by some kind of gas pumped through his mail slot. When he awakes, he staggers uncertainly to the window and opens the blinds. He looks below to the central square of "The Village," a fantastic collection of eccentric buildings, alleyways and parks on a verdant hillside beside a sandy, crescent bay.

His name, never actually spoken during the series, is now Number 6, and the unknown captors, led by Number 2, demand to know why he's resigned. He vows never to tell, and the sequence ends with him running wildly on a moonlit beach. He thrusts his fist in the air and gives the now-famous battle cry: "I am not a number, I am a free man!"

Spoiler Alert.

What follows are mini plot summaries of all 17 episodes. If you haven't yet seen the series, and are planning to, and don't want anything given away, please skip down to *Six Of One*.

The opening episode is magnificent. Simply called *Arrival*, it establishes the premise and sets the stylistic tone for the series. More expository than action-packed, as befits its role as chapter one, *Arrival* still manages to convey a sinister mood as our hero progressively susses out his predicament, attempts a few tentative escapes, learns he can trust no one, and meets not one but two Number 2s. And right off the bat we experience one of *The Prisoner's* recurring hallmarks: an obsessive attention to detail.

In *Free For All* Number 6, in order to meet the mysterious Number 1, runs for election as the new Number 2. Written and directed by McGoohan, this episode features a scathing attack on the democratic election process, as well as the warning to Number 6 that his captors can break him in many ways, and will use both mental and physical torture to achieve their ends.

Dance of the Dead combines brainwashing and the legal system, in which a predominantly female cast (including a cat) attempt to break Number 6 against the incongruous background of a carnival. After breaking the rules by taking a transistor radio from a body that washed up on the shore, Number 6 is subjected to a kangaroo trial and he discovers just how easily crowds can be swayed. He eludes the angry crowd of villagers and ends up in a room containing a teletype machine which, incongruously, seems to be the low-tech communication link between the Village and Number 1. This episode appears to be heavily influenced by Orson Wells, with the chase under the Town Hall lifted almost exactly from Well's film of Kafka's *The Trial*.

Checkmate features a human chessboard, with Number 6 as Queen's pawn. A rook runs amok and is taken away for aversion therapy for being an "individual," but Number 6 thinks he might still be a willing co-escapee. Number 6 is also intrigued by Number 14, who believes he can tell between prisoners and warders by their attitude of either subservience or arrogance. Betting that inmates would do as they were told, and warders would not, Number 6 assembles a gang and plots an escape by sea. When he boards the rescue boat, Number 6 receives a unexpected surprise—a television monitor shows the face of Number 2, and Number 6 has been caught in his own trap. His own arrogance has convinced his co-conspirators that he was a warder attempting to trick them.

The Chimes of Big Ben reveals why Number 6 can be called an escape artist. His ingenious woodcarving, appropriately called *Escape*, allows him and a new prisoner, the beautiful Number 8, to sail away from The Village. After months of travel he reaches what appears to be the London office of the organization he quit. Just before he starts to answer their questions, Big Ben chimes, and Number 6 realizes all is not as it seems.

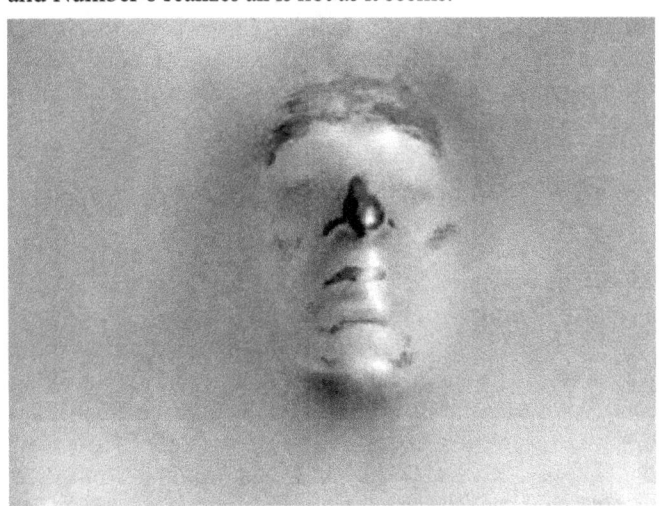

In *A, B, and C* Number 2 invades Number 6's dreams in an attempt to discover why he resigned. Each letter refers to a potion which triggers a dream featuring one of the three people Number 6 might confide in about his retirement. Great premise. Great ending.

The General is a warning about educational methods. A form of subliminal speed learning deposits information into the mind, but what is the value of facts without understanding? Number 6 foils the "General"—a room-sized computer—in a manner reminiscent of Capt. Kirk of *Star Trek*.

In *The Schizoid Man* McGoohan plays two roles—as Number 6 and also as his double, Number 12. Number 6 undergoes extensive brainwashing and is told he is Number 12. His assignment is to pose as Number 6's double to make himself believe he is Number 12; in turn, his double claims that he is the real Number 6. Which is which? Turns out you have to be a mind reader to tell.

Many Happy Returns is another escape plot—Number 6 awakens to a deserted Village, builds a raft, and finally makes it back to his home and car in London. He convinces his former employers of the fact of The Village, and searches for it by jet. When they find it, the pilot says the usual Village good-bye: "Be seeing you," to the shocked Number 6, who is ejected from the airplane and parachutes back into the Village.

In *It's Your Funeral* Number 6 finds himself involved in thwarting an assassination plot against a retiring Number 2 by the replacement Number 2. We meet the "Jammers"—people who continually pass on false and alarmist warnings to deliberately confuse the authorities—and we are introduced to "Kosho," a trampoline-based game invented by McGoohan which involves a lot of jumping around while trying to push your opponent into a tank of water. Overall, a confusing, unsatisfying episode.

In *A Change of Mind* Number 6 still refuses to join the village community and finds himself accused by a citizen committee of being a "rebel," "reactionary" and "disharmonious." Number 6 is declared "unmutual" and is subjected to "instant social conversion"—a pre-frontal lobotomy performed by Number 48, a woman doctor, and the operation is shown on the Village's closed circuit television. Afterwards, he appears to be a changed man, tranquil and non-aggressive, which the Villagers applaud as his "social conversion." Number 6 later tricks Number 48 into admitting his operation was faked and that the illusion was maintained by the use of drugs. Number 6, now completely in control of himself, gives her a post-hypnotic order which turns the tables on Number 2.

In *Hammer Into Anvil* Number 2 tortures Number 73 until she leaps from a window. Number 6 vows revenge and leads Number 2 into a state of paranoia so devastating he reports himself to Number 1.

Mind switching is the basis of *Do Not Forsake Me, Oh My Darling*. Number 6 wakes in his London flat to discover his mind in another man's body. A missing scientist is found, there's a lot more mind switching, and a neat twist at the end. The plot meant McGoohan didn't have to be on the set, and this break in the action allowed him to fly to the USA, where he filmed his role in the movie, *Ice Station Zebra*.

Living in Harmony, the first Western ever to be filmed for television in the UK, starts with a Western parody of the usual

episode-starting resignation. A man, dressed in Western gear, rides into town and turns in his Sheriff's badge. When he walks away he's attacked by a gang of cowboys and is dragged to a town called Harmony. After western adventures and a vicious gunfight in which he takes a bullet in the head, Number 6 awakens to find himself back in the Village, surrounded by cardboard cutouts of Western trappings. Clearly he's been drugged and made to act out the whole thing. This episode was not shown in the US as it was considered inappropriate to show a non-combatant/peacenick during the Vietnam War. Amazing, no?

The Girl Who Was Death follows, a spy spoof featuring Justine Lord as a girl who believes she and Number 6 were made for each other—he is a born survivor and she is a born killer. Her methods are hilarious, and range from an explosive-filled cricket ball to poisoned drinks in a bar. It gets even better—her father thinks he's Napoleon and they live in a lighthouse that's actually a rocket aimed at London. Number 6 cleverly foils their plans. "And that is how I saved London from the mad scientist," says Number 6. He's been reading the story to two Village children while Number 2 and his cronies listen in. A nod to the antics of *The Avengers*.

By contrast, the penultimate episode, *Once Upon A Time*, is a brutal psychological battle to the death between Number 6 and Number 2 (brilliantly played by Leo McKern). At night, Number 6 is brainwashed by Number 2. He sings him nursery rhymes and when Number 6 awakes, his mind has regressed back to childhood. Number 6 fights back, however, and as Number 2 weakens he becomes more desperate, and finally dies. Number 6 has won his freedom, and the chance to meet the mysterious Number 1.

This is the order in which A&E presents *The Prisoner*, and there is still much controversy over the exact order in which the series should be watched, as McGoohan *et al* were required to hastily develop more plots to meet Lew Grade's requirement for 26 shows. Thirteen were made for the first year (McGoohan says four plots were developed "over a weekend," and when the premise began wearing thin, and viewership dropped, it was decided to end the series.

The Final Episode, *Fall Out*.

Once Upon A Time segues neatly into the final, controversial episode, *Fall Out*. In many ways this episode is a story unto itself, and deserves its own analysis. Either brilliant or inane, McGoohan was given very few days to wrap up the series, and wrote this episode in complete secrecy. When it was shown, to a record audience, it made headline news because of the controversy it created. The negative reaction was so intense that people apparently besieged McGoohan's house and he had to leave London for a few weeks.

It is a wacky story.

Continuing on from *Once Upon A Time*, Number 6 is taken by the Supervisor and the ubiquitous mini-Butler to meet Number 1. He enters a large chamber. One wall is covered with technical equipment, another contains a semi-circular seating area filled with 20 hooded and robed figures, each representing a Village association or interest group. They wear hideous masks, painted half-black, half-white.

In the centre of the room sits a presiding Judge (Kenneth Griffith). Military police are all round the chamber and a teeter-totter holding men with machine guns revolves beside vapour-filled holes in the floor. We also see a cylindrical metal wall with a mechanical glass eye (shades of HAL).

The Judge gives a long, rambling speech, and a young

man (Alexis Kenner), Number 48, is brought up from a pit and lectured. Number 48 replies using an odd mixture of hip slang and breaks into song—an old negro spiritual called *Dem Bones*.

The dead Number 2 is then resurrected, (revealing a continuity problem, as McKern is revived with shorter hair, trimmed beard, and less weight!—turns out *Fall Out* was shot months after *Once Upon A Time*). Number 6 is given his name back—"sir"—a million dollars in traveler's cheques, his passport and keys to his London home and car, and is then invited to address the masked audience. His speech is inexplicably drowned out by the masked crowd's chanting. The Judge now gives him the opportunity to meet Number 1, and they descend

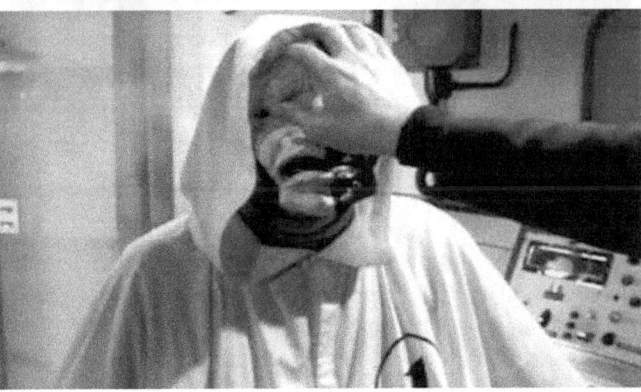

into the basement, past the imprisoned Numbers 2 and 48, and up a circular metal staircase. Number 6 finds himself in a room full of equipment—and simple globes of the earth—and a masked, hooded figure who hands him a crystal ball. Number 6 takes it, notices the figure is wearing the Number 1 badge, and drops the ball. He pulls off Number 1's mask to reveal the face of an ape. Shades of Charles Darwin? The ape face, too, is a mask, and pulling it off, Number 6 reveals his own face! Number 1 is Number 6? But this face is of an id-like Number 6, who hoots and cackles and dances around like a demented child before fleeing the room. Really, one must think, is this heavy-handed or what?

Number 6 returns to the control room and starts flipping switches. We now discover the whole complex is also the interior of a rocket, and Number 6 has triggered the launch sequence. The upper chamber panics and a mass evacuation of the entire Village begins.

Going back down the spiral staircase, Number 6 knocks out the guards, releases Numbers 2 and 48 and, with the help of the Butler, returns to the central chamber where a gun battle breaks out. After killing the guards, they escape in the detachable cage—seen in *Once Upon A Time* and actually the back of a truck— and crash out through an underground tunnel. Our last shot of the Village shows the rocket blasting slowly skyward.

Magically, the escapees find themselves on the A20 freeway heading for London. After throwing the contents of the cage onto the road, Number 48, preferring to take his chances alone, gets off the truck and hitchhikes. Number 2 gets off beside the Houses of Parliament, and Number 6 returns to his home with the Butler. The Butler walks to the door, which opens by itself. A telling action, as all the doors in the Village also opened by themselves. Number 6 gets into his car and drives away. After a clap of thunder, he is seen driving on a runway exactly as he was in the opening title sequence.

Brilliant Or Inane?

Regardless of its artistic merit, one has to admit *Fall Out* is one very unique hour of television. I'm not sure if any other show had self-consciously "ended" itself prior to this series, but even if it had gone out with a special series-wrapping ending, I'm sure the point would have been to answer the show's major questions, not muddy the waters even further.

The genius of McGoohan notwithstanding, in the final analysis, this last episode is a confused and confusing cloudbank of ethereal ideas and what appears to be sleep-deprived imagery. The images in *Fall Out* simply pile higher and higher upon each other until the whole thing morphs into incomprehensibility. The trial. The costumes. The slave song. The final meeting and madness of the Number 1/Number 6 revelation.

Throughout the entire series no one, audience or participant, knew the identity of Number 1. I'm not saying McGoohan should have pandered to his audience and presented them with an evil, James Bond-type enemy—too much of a cliché after all these adventures involving the individual (Number 6) *vs* various challengers (all the other Numbers, plus non-Villagers). But now we have the final showdown, the face to face meeting of the well-known protagonist and unknown antagonist— the good and the bad, the principled and the pragmatic—not opposed, but blended into mirror images.

What to make of this? If Number 1 and Number 6 look the same, but certainly don't act the same, then McGoohan is revealing the irony of all of us trying to escape, essentially, ourselves. This Mobius Strip of McGoohan philosophy, able to mysteriously combine two surfaces into one, is at least a novel idea, and one which deserves a far better treatment than the merry *melange* of ideas we're offered in *Fall-Out,* which surely must be a title with many meanings.

Six Of One…

So, what is it that makes *The Prisoner* a cult classic after all these years? I can think of six reasons:

The Creative Team. There was a lot of magic in the original crew of McGoohan, producer David Tomblin, story editor George Markstein and art director Jack Shampan. All had worked together on *Danger Man*, so they knew each other well, and each in turn had a willing group of equally talented people at their call. Given that magic combination of little time and lots of money, they successfully synthesized a concept which turned out to be far greater than the sum of the parts.

The Basic Premise. Start with a great concept: someone resigns as a spy, is captured and incarcerated in a remote area, and

clever attempts are made to make the spy confess and blend in with the prison population. Spiff it up with The Village, the endless parade of new Number 2s, the science fiction elements, the enigma of Number 1, and the apparent eventual triumph of the individual, and you have a great platform upon which compelling stories can be told. Beneath all that glitter, though, lies the real gold: the very basic premise is that we're all prisoners, you and I, and we're prisoners of our own device. Hell is ironic, apparently.

The Acting Talent. Aside from McGoohan, who delivers in virtually every episode, the series tapped a wide range of the best journeymen actors in the UK at the time. Leo McKern is exceptionally good, as is Alexis Kanner, who appeared three times in the 17 episodes. McGoohan is brilliant at the McGoohan "look"—that peer-slightly-up-to-the-camera stare, flashing eyes beaming out at you under those deep eyebrows, the confident challenge with an ironic smirk that suitably unnerves all within its glare. The slightly singsong voice, dulcet tones, and flashes of violent activity make him the embodiment of Number 6.

Style And Substance. Not only were the stories unique, but the way in which The Prisoner was shot was also groundbreaking. The clipped speeches work perfectly with the series' trademark fast zooms, upfront sound effects, compelling music, bright lighting, long shots and ubiquitous quick cuts, used most effectively in the verbally violent interrogation scenes. Then there's the dichotomy of the Victorian pennyfarthing bicycle and eccentric Village architecture, set against the high-tech underworld of Number 2 and the deadly Rover.

The Art Direction. Jack Shampan should have won awards for his role in the design of The Prisoner. Although the resort at Hotel Portmeirion had already been scouted by McGoohan years earlier when he was shooting *Danger Man*, the careful attention to detail, the costumes, the cage-like look of the control centre, the underground sets, all contributed to the overall believability of the outrageous plots. Of course, it helped that he had such a generous budget to work with.

The Endless Enigmas. Truly, no series before or after has ever asked and left unanswered so many questions: Who is Number 6? Why did Number 6 resign? Where is The Village? Who controls The Village? And, most importantly, Who is Number 1? The lack of obvious answers—it's strange that the Number 6 is Number 1 shocker of *Fall Out* is resisted or ignored by most commentators—has left this series open-ended, and unresolved means many, many people have undertaken the equally-enigmatic task of trying to make sense of the whole zany exercise.

Half Dozen Of The Other...

Of course, what made this series great also holds its seeds of destruction. Talk about watch and irony. There is much about *The Prisoner* that is clumsy and irritating:

The McGoohan Factor. No matter what the creative roles of the senior team, *The Prisoner* is, essentially, McGoohan's baby. Although *The Prisoner* is culturally linked to the liberal, permissive 60s, McGoohan's sympathies were not with revolting, anti-war leftist students and advocates of sex, drugs and rock'n'roll. "He was very puritanical," according to co-star Alexis Kanner. "In *Living In Harmony* we had to put a shadow over some dead girl's breasts. Patrick had come down and everybody knew he'd disapprove. I mean, he turned down James Bond. They offered him $10 million, and I happen to know this is true, just to come and talk to them about playing Bond."

This puritanical aspect is revealed in many ways: the series is full of gorgeous (for the times) babes, but Number 6 is loath to even touch a woman, much less romance her. Markstein accuses McGoohan of a proclivity to playing roles in which he plays god, and certainly Number 6 assumes a godlike role, chastely plotting the defeat of all satanic Number 2s (the last one even dies), and then freeing himself in the final episode to the tune of that gospel classic, *Dem Bones*. It is generally conceded that McGoohan's attempt to go from actor to producer/writer/director/editor— God—is fraught with many missteps.

The Basic Premise. As McGoohan discovers, it's easy to generate seven shows based on the series' original premise, but it's not so easy to string it out for 17 episodes. The ten fillers tend to veer away from the mind *vs* mind of the spy *vs* spy premise to venture into social commentary, with such inferior forms as satires (education, politics), spoofs (other spy shows), and allegory (a western). Trouble is, the Basic Premise of *The Prisoner* is simply the battle we fight within ourselves between good and evil, represented by the so-called Free Man and Repressive Society— one can almost hear Freud nattering away in *Civilisation and its Discontents*. Can an institution break an individual to the point where he betrays himself? Well, if the series is to continue on next week, of course it can't. So McGoohan is reduced to dreaming up all the various ways Number 6 might be threatened, but never defeated. Suspense is impossible, so the recourse is cleverness. Ah, and what a difficult course that is to maintain.

The Rover Syndrome. The death-dealing beach ball takes on *deus ex machina* roles far too often, and seems to exist mainly to keep the Villagers from simply wandering away

into the surrounding countryside. The fact it can kill makes it as menacing as the roar which announces its arrival. In the original plan, Rover was to be a crumpet-shaped vehicle that could climb walls, float and dive in the sea. It showed up for the first day of shooting, was driven into the ocean, and promptly sank.

Legend has it that while McGoohan was standing on the beach, pondering his next move, production manager Bernie Williams looked in the sky and saw a weather balloon. He pointed it out to McGoohan, who told him to get one so they could look at it. They apparently went thru about 6,000 of them during the entire series. "They easily broke," explains Williams, but they still figured out all the ways to make it move with seeming intelligence.

One could make the argument that it, too, represents the "old-fashioned" in the same sinister way as the ever-present bicycle, but it is one of many science fiction oddities that far outpace in technical skills the rest of the Village's laughably antiquated computer systems. Bottom line, much of the science fiction in *The Prisoner* would still be a marvel today, and is much too magical for the most of *The Prisoner's* technological paraphernalia.

The Idiot Enigmas. Even a cursory sweep of the web reveals an amazing number of major *Prisoner* sites, and all, it seems, are fixated on propounding theories about the True Meaning of the series. One could probably argue that the concept of never tying up any loose ends may constitute the basis of an elliptical style, but *The Prisoner* often seems willing to take advantage of the human desire to create order out of chaos, and is only too willing to supply the chaos from which the theories spring. McGoohan is quoted as saying he wanted the series to generate discussion— and he certainly achieved that goal. But one wonders where the line is crossed between good story telling, and simple audience manipulation. The question of whether or not Number 6 is John Drake from *Danger Man* is moot and immaterial; the point is that Number 6 symbolizes an almost Wilsonian outsider, a Randian superman of higher consciousness and inflexible will—with wit and a strong jawline to match. Number 6 is the audience, after all, fulfilling the time-honoured role of hero, offering us the omnipotent point-of-view. McGoohan himself has said numerous times that John Drake is not Number 6, but there are practical economic reasons for this, because if Number 6 were referred to as John Drake, royalties would have to be paid out to Ralph Smart, the creator and producer of *Danger Man*.

Why Did Number 6 Really Resign? Numbers 2 come and go with alarming regularity, vainly trying to find that answer, but ultimately, why do they care so much? Throughout the series, Number 6 offers a number of vague or unenthusiastic answers, and why? What's the big deal about telling Number 2 you quit because you just didn't want to be a secret agent any more? One is tempted to think up much more interesting questions for an agent of Number 6's stature, but this whole question of "resignation" takes one back to Markstein, who wrote the original series premise and the first episode, and has gone on record as being very pissed that McGoohan resigned as *Danger Man*, throwing most of his colleagues out of work. *Arrival* states that Number 2's superiors see Number 6's knowledge as a very valuable commodity, and one ultimately suspects they're just as likely to kill Number 6 as having him confess—for, even if he does confess, he is still doomed to live out the rest of his days in the Village.

Where is The Village? Again, who really cares? True, Number 6 threatens to escape, return and blow the joint up, and ultimately does destroy it in *Fall Out*. Is the Village anything more that what it symbolizes—the "outward and visible sign" of the inner evils of a repressive society? In the dualism of the series, the Village happily adds an old-fashioned, visually exciting backdrop to the exterior shots, thereby neatly offsetting the interior shots—the futuristic cages of technology which surround Number 2 and his/her cronies. McGoohan further muddies the waters in a clumsy way: the location of The Village is part of the plot in three episodes of *The Prisoner*. In each episode, the location shifts wildly. Bad story editing, or deliberate attempt to confuse?

What's with the Episode Order? This is just plain silly. Nobody knows the exact order in which the 17 episodes should be viewed. Episodes one, 16 and 17 are obviously correct in the sequence, but after that it becomes vague. *Free For All* and *Dance Of The Dead* feature speeches which date them as early episodes, and after that it's a guessing game. Why? Because production was very late on a tight schedule, and episodes were broadcast in the order they were completed, not the order in which they were written. This A&E boxed set actually has a little paragraph under each episode description, entitled "Episode Order Debate," which attempts to justify why this particular episode is given its particular slot. The seven core episodes which McGoohan says "really count" are (in his order): *Arrival, Free For All, Dance of the Dead, Checkmate, The Chimes of Big Ben, Once Upon a Time* and *Fall Out*.

Who Controls The Village? Number 6 continually asks this question, is never overtly answered, and much discussion has ensued: capitalists or communists? Watching the series today, it seems obvious the Village is culturally a British invention, and Number 6's tormentors are his ex-employers.

The Orson Wells Does Kafka Connection. One doesn't have to be a scholar of literature to think of connections between *The Prisoner* and Franz Kafka. After all, any story which deals with alienation and the incomprehensibilities of the bureaucratic state must ultimately pay homage to the Great unMaster himself.

In this case, however, the homage is slightly less direct: there are numerous visual parallels between *The Prisoner* and the Orson Wells' cinematic version of *The Trial*, starring Anthony Perkins. McGoohan reportedly has high respect for Wells, but any question of direct inspiration for *The Prisoner* falls directly into the camp of endless speculation, which continues to surround *The Prisoner* like a fog of intellect. Or Kafkian action.

It Means What It Is.

What makes *The Prisoner* so special? Ironically, it's probably its complexity and confusion—the same things that make it incomprehensible to, and therefore unpopular with, much of its original and subsequent audiences.

One suspects that the chaos of production, the unquestioned subjectivity of McGoohan's artistic vision, the unstructured way in which it embraces different concepts from all sorts of philosophic directions, and the way it avoids easy classification—all this gives *The Prisoner* its enduring intellectual charm.

One suspects that if everything had been professionally planned and executed, and that if George Markstein had been able to keep the series on the "strict reality" path which was originally intended for it, then *The Prisoner* might have turned out to be just another TV series—well made, quite interesting, but safe and ordinary—just like *Danger Man*.

Ultimately, questions about what *The Prisoner* is about isn't what *The Prisoner* is about. It doesn't have to make specific sense; it doesn't have to mean anything. As we learn at the art exhibition in *Chimes of Big Ben*:

An Art Judge: "We're not quite sure what it means."
Number 6: "It means what it is."

Precisely. In the biggest picture of all, probably only two points need to be made: the prisoner is a prisoner of his own making, and the prisoner will remain a prisoner, for all of us contain good and evil, a prisoner and a jailor. Remind you of the endless battle twixt Eros and Thanatos? Perhaps it's fitting that nobody *wins*.

Incarcerate Yourself.

Confusing or nay, *The Prisoner* at its best offers some superb story lines, well-written, well-shot, well-directed, well-edited, and yes, well-acted. Episodes which stand out as high-water marks include *Chimes of Big Ben*, with its brilliant plot; *The Schizoid Man*, again, very original; *Many Happy Returns*, with its silent beginning; *A, B, and C*, which has probably the best ending of all 17 episodes, and *Arrival*, which eerily sets the stage and introduces our characters.

"I suppose that *The Prisoner* is the sort of thing where a thousand people might have a different interpretation of it, which I think is very gratifying. I am glad that's the way it was because that was the intention"—Patrick McGoohan.

Congratulations, Patrick. Your intention worked. No doubt better than you ever imagined.

You've already been parodied on *The Simpsons*.

Sam Fuller: Shocking Corridor

Toronto, 2001

HERE'S ANOTHER CLASSIC MOVIE I reviewed for the website *Culture Court* in 2001. And what a film! *Shock Corridor* is the aptly named 1963 B-movie psychodrama from the vigorously independent mind of American film auteur Samuel Fuller.

This movie tells the fascinating story of Johnny Barrett, a fame-obsessed, big city newspaper reporter who is fixated on winning the Pulitzer Prize. His plan is daring: by masquerading as a sexual deviant, he'll gain entry to the local state mental hospital, mingle with the patients, crack an unsolved murder case, and write his prize-winning story—all while never realizing the terrible price he must pay.

What makes this movie brilliant—a masterpiece—is the incredible manner in which Fuller takes this basic story of one man's overwhelming desire for fame and recognition and extrapolates it allegorically, creating a powerful parable that reveals this seat-squirming truth: if one man can be destroyed by an absorption into irrational thoughts, so can an entire society. Once you admit America is one big asylum, then it's hard to tell the sane from the crazy when we're all walking down that same symbolic corridor.

Fuller sees an America driven by a morality which says the ends justify the means, managed by the corporate alienation of big institutions—represented by the newspaper, the asylum, the psychiatric establishment and its bureaucracy of shrinks and staff. Against this dark, disjointed background Fuller props up his two protagonists: the egotistical, aggressive Johnny and his sexy yet conservative girlfriend, the stripper Cathy. As Fuller's metaphors for America they represent a potent shopping list of psychopathologic ingredients. Just wait until you see how Fuller mixmasters the two into this jaw-dropping rant on the mental state of America.

Whom God Wishes to Destroy—He First Turns Mad.

Fuller bookends this film with the famous Euripides quote, just one of many intellectual references he makes throughout the movie—Hamlet, Freudian psychology, Dickens—which must have further widened the gap between the movie and its probably-uneducated audience. The trailer which comes with the DVD hypes this film as "incredibly realistic," clinically diagnoses the main characters, shows quick clips of virtually all the sex and violence, and promises an evening

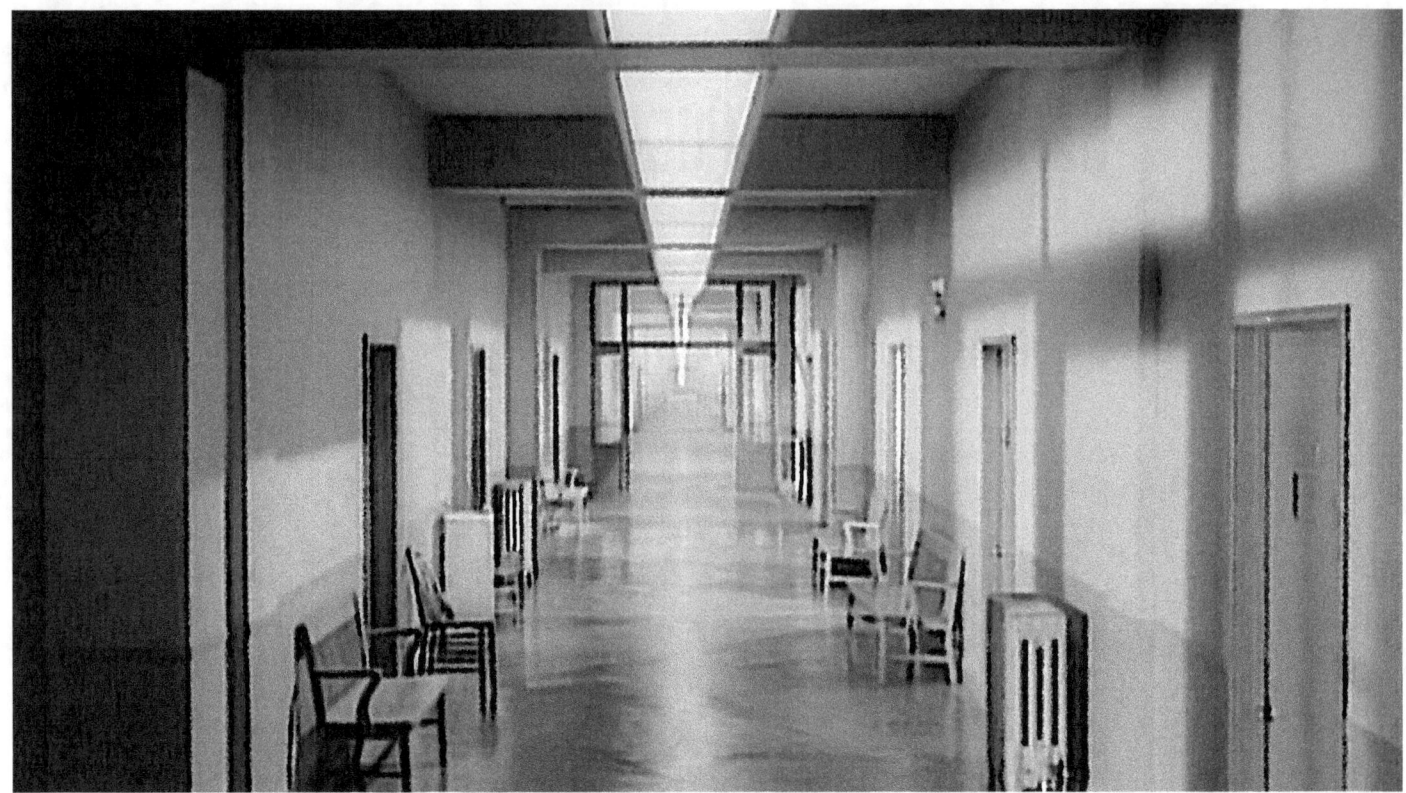

of entertainment that "Breaks The Shock Barrier!" with the "Biggest Jolt!" Audiences sucked in by this taboo-laden trailer must have been extraordinarily shocked by what they were actually shown. Rather than gasping in shock at nothing but the violent antics of sex-mad crazies, they found themselves in an aggressive allegory, no doubt vaguely worried that all the mayhem on the screen might have a deeper, more sinister meaning. It does. *Shock Corridor* was made in 1963. Today, that era is the "Camelot" period of U.S. history—those youthful, self-confident days before the execution of Kennedy, the politics of Vietnam and British rock music. In reality, 1963 America was vainly attempting to ignore a lot of stressful, "slow drip" problems—the world was in the depths of the Cold War, and the public was still having nightmares from the close call of the Cuban embargo.

In the south, simmering racial tension was about to boil over into the first shocking national TV coverage of race riots, protest marches, Martin Luther King and the national guard. It was the perfect time for independent filmmakers like Sam Fuller to challenge audiences with meaning rather than with escape.

Fuller's warning is the obverse of Euripides: because America is mad, that's proof of God's plan to destroy it. *Shock Corridor* offers a series of sociopathic proofs to back Fuller's then-radical assertion.

Proof #1: The Place. The movie's central symbol is the asylum's main corridor, ironically called "The Street" by the guard-like staff. You don't have to have the blues to see it's one lonely avenue. It's starkly clinical. Lined with hard, wooden park benches. Interrupted with big water heating units. The harsh lighting beats down over all, emphasizing the sense of black and white, sane and insane. There is no grey area of compromise or understanding. There are no plants, no hint of growth or life or nurturing. There is no art, no imagination, no meanings, no sign of intellectual curiosity.

The Street is the centre of the asylum, and Fuller blatantly elevates it to represent Main Street, USA.

Proof #2: The People. Johnny and Cathy not only guide the plot, but they supply the sexual deviance required by B-movie protocol. One could argue that Johnny's implied sexual problems are no doubt the basis for his compulsive dreams of wealth and power. Is he impotent? He seems immune to Cathy's charms before he gains access to the asylum, and once in, he begins to confuse the sexual Cathy (his girlfriend) with the

non-sexual Cathy (she pretends to be his sister). Here's a man suffering from "erotic dementia", who basically runs from sexual encounters throughout the entire movie.

Cathy is equally confused. She talks a good game when justifying her job as a stripper, needs the money, blah, blah, blah—but she still needs the attention of strange men, and craves the lascivious stares her body attracts. She seems overly fond of a pink boa, and likes to click around in form-revealing outfits. This objectification of herself into a soft porn commodity also seems to be a flight from an open, warm relationship, and as such reveals much about her attraction to the sexually-neutral Johnny. Quite the barren couple.

Cathy uses exhibitionism to earn admiration, and for Johnny, winning some prestigious prize will fulfill his need for recognition—the refuge of all troubled with low self-esteem. His plan is to live off this glory for the rest of his life—"there will be a book in this—a play—maybe even a movie." How ironic can you get? That he loses when he wins is god-like punishment for his (and America's) hubris: we see him finally—as the sadistic Dr. Menkin indelicately observes—as "an insane mute with the Pulitzer Prize." Poetic justice, or not?

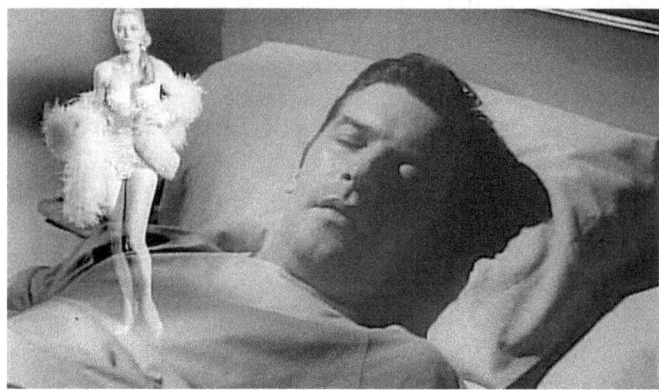

Proof #3: The Patients. In a stroke of genius, Fuller creates three patients to represent three themes on the madness of America: xenophobia, racism, and nuclear war. Johnny seeks each out to interview them about the murder, hoping to uncover the killer's identity, but what he really discovers is the method of madness: psychosis as the ultimate prozac, the best way to avoid a painful reality. Shades of Pink Floyd. It's part of the grim irony of *Shock Corridor* that Johnny, fixated on solving the murder, misses his chance to write a "real" Pulitzer Prize winning story about the sad lives of these three patients—Stuart, Dr Boden, and Trent—who are ultimately the raison d'être of the movie. Here are three empty canvasses ready for Fuller to paint with broad, insistent, punishing strokes. Ultimately, the content of each portrait is the same: each victim has morphed into an ironic antithesis of their prior selves. Welcome to the Land of the Oppressed and the Home of the Meek.

Meet Stuart, a simple southerner, unfortunately raised on a continual diet of venom by his xenophobic parents, brainwashed to hate until he was "ready to defect to anyone". Captured and converted to communism during the Korean war, Stuart helped to brainwash captured Americans until one of them brainwashed him back to America. He returns, is ostracized as a social outcast, and retreats into insanity, mentally re-fighting the Civil War as Southern General Jeb Stuart, plotting campaigns in which Americans kill other Americans—over ideology. Some things never change!

We also meet Dr. Boden, a genius formerly involved in the development of the atomic bomb. Smart guy who likes to play with equations? Fine. Fuller takes him back to being a six-year-old child, happy to crayon and play hide-and-seek. Through Boden's child-like speeches Fuller points his accusing finger at the then-current gamesmanship of mutually assured destruction (MAD) between the US and Russia.

However, the most startling of all Fuller's patients is Trent, the first black student ever admitted to an all-white Southern university. Imagine the pressure. He can't just be average, he has to be better than his fellow white students. He also has to avoid the hissing wall of hatred that lurks on the periphery of every moment he's in the enemy camp. This burden soon grinds Trent into his own psychic overload, and his escape is classic.

Rather than buying an Uzi and spreading his tormentor's brains over the ivy-covered walls, Trent decides his enemies were right: white is superior. He anoints himself Grand Wizard of the KKK and passes his time making hoods out of stolen pillowcases, inciting attacks upon other black inmates, and ranting racist monologues.

Incredibly, he makes a catatonic patient hold up his arm in a Nazi salute and points out that it looks like the Statue of Liberty. Heavy. Fuller's twist of pulling the usual white supremist propaganda out of the mouth of a black man is pure genius. The scene in which Trent is introduced is one of the movie's most effective high points—the audience hears the litany of racist hatred long before Fuller reveals Trent's face. The gasps from the audience are audible.

Stylistically, *Shock Corridor* is a visual treat. With Fuller in complete control, he takes advantage of the stark cinematography of Stanley Cortez (*The Magnificent Ambersons, Night of the Hunter*). He keeps the camera moving, from middle to tight shots, to heighten the psychological reactions of his characters, allowing their close-ups to show the angst and ennui that the cheap sets can only augment.

The acting in this movie is very well done. Peter Breck plays the puffed up Johnny to perfection, and you'll be wide-eyed with mirth at his barely controlled, over-the-top attempts at fake insanity. And equally amused at his under-the-top attempts at real insanity. Breck is able to capture Johnny's slide into deep psychosis in a finely-paced performance, climaxing in an incredible corridor scene where he runs from closed door to closed door as the hard rain pelts down and the lightning crashes around him. He seems able to get inside Johnny's obsessions and is very good when he notices events and quotes headlines for his planned crime exposé. Manic.

Constance Towers is statuesque as Cathy the stripper, and aside from driveling over Johnny, her most memorable scene is the early strip tease, in which she doffs no duds and offers a truly remarkable dance routine. An adequate actress, she no doubt benefits greatly from being married to Fuller—especially as he tends to stay on her close-ups just a tad too long.

Hari Rhodes gives a spectacular performance as the black-hating black, Trent. James Best is very believable as Stuart, the good ole General, and Gene Evans is well-cast as Boden. The corridor plays itself to perfection, thanks to the film's Art Director, Eugene Laurie. The parable form works especially well in this world of high contrast, black and white images. You'll see lots of noir light angling across faces and walls, lots of shadows, bright lights, deep gloom. There's a surprising number of complex, drawn out fight scenes, and plenty of fast-paced, physical action, featuring aggressive, in-your-face shots and cuts, multi-layered special visual effects, and, of course, the usual sprinkling of suspect cuts. Just what you want.

Shock Corridor is also famous for one unique Fullerism. It's a B&W film, but during their conversations with Johnny, all three murder witnesses comment upon and then describe little color "dream" fantasy sequences. Their dreams? Little chunks of amateurish 16mm footage Fuller took for another film! He simply writes appropriate dialogue to explain the strange inclusion of footage of Mt. Fuji, Buddhists, Amazon warriors, trains—all of which add a *Wizard of Oz* jolt to otherwise pedestrian footage. But there's more. According to Victoria-based movie critic Panos Cosmatos, the Amazon tribes color clips used by Fuller in *Shock Corridor* were originally shot in 1954 for a film called *Tigrero*, which was to star John Wayne. That film was never made, but Fuller went back to the jungle and showed the film he had made in 1954 to the same natives 40 years later. He made that trip into a 1995 documentary called *Tigrero: A Film That Was Never Made*.

You can almost see Fuller figuring out this movie. He decides to do a social commentary on contemporary culture... *fine, let's pick the cold war, racism, and hatred. Better throw in a little sex... a few more bums in the seats. Fuller used to be a journalist... good, he'll make the hero a reporter... they can nose around... man, this is crazy stuff... that's it... let's make in an asylum movie.* It's like he came up withall the basic themes, then dreamed up the zany crime plot as a device to get everyone together in the nut house so he can whack us over the head with his real message. Truly, this is a look at society through grimy glasses. But ultimately, it's all mind and no matter, because when Johnny starts to lose the bricks from his wall, his search for the killer essentially fades into irrelevance. By the end, Johnny's obsessive quest is only a cipher, a road sign in his exploration of the endless corridor in which his mind is trapped. The irony is cool: the closer he comes to success, the sicker he becomes—until, triumphant at the end, Johnny slips into his new role as chief copywriter for the quiet city of Catatonia. For America, the message is loud and clear. Sometimes, the ends don't justify the means.

What makes this movie so compelling is the imaginative way in which Fuller reveals his themes. Like the folk music/beatnik subcultures of the day, this allegory is an exercise in finger-pointing, and Fuller maximizes the complete range of his substantial talents to create a masterpiece of indictment on the sorry state of Cold War America.

Bottom line, *Shock Corridor* is that rare exploitation flick which achieves masterpiece status. While it contains the usual taboos of the B-movies of that era—a burlesque musical number, a brutal attack by a gang of cannibalistic nymphomaniacs, the suggestion of incest, and the mandatory electroshock sequence—the genius of *Shock Corridor* is Fuller's daring, revolutionary portrayal of what he sees as dystopian in society. It was a tense, irrational time—spoofed to perfection in such later movies as *Dr. Strangelove*—and Fuller takes full advantage of the psychopathologic Gestalt, using the genre of the asylum film to offer up a powerful, unique vision in a commercial medium rarely used for such strong social criticism. Even in today's culture Fuller's revelations about how society can make you insane still booms clearly when violence, armed with high-tech guns and Second Chance body armor, erupts on our main streets and in our schools.

The list is still in place: race hatred, gun worship, escapist entertainment, compulsive obsessions. One wonders why this film hasn't been redone, updated to re-examine the escalating madness of today's America. As one of the asylum staff tells Johnny: "We're here to help you to remember not to forget."

Maybe we're ready for another reminder.

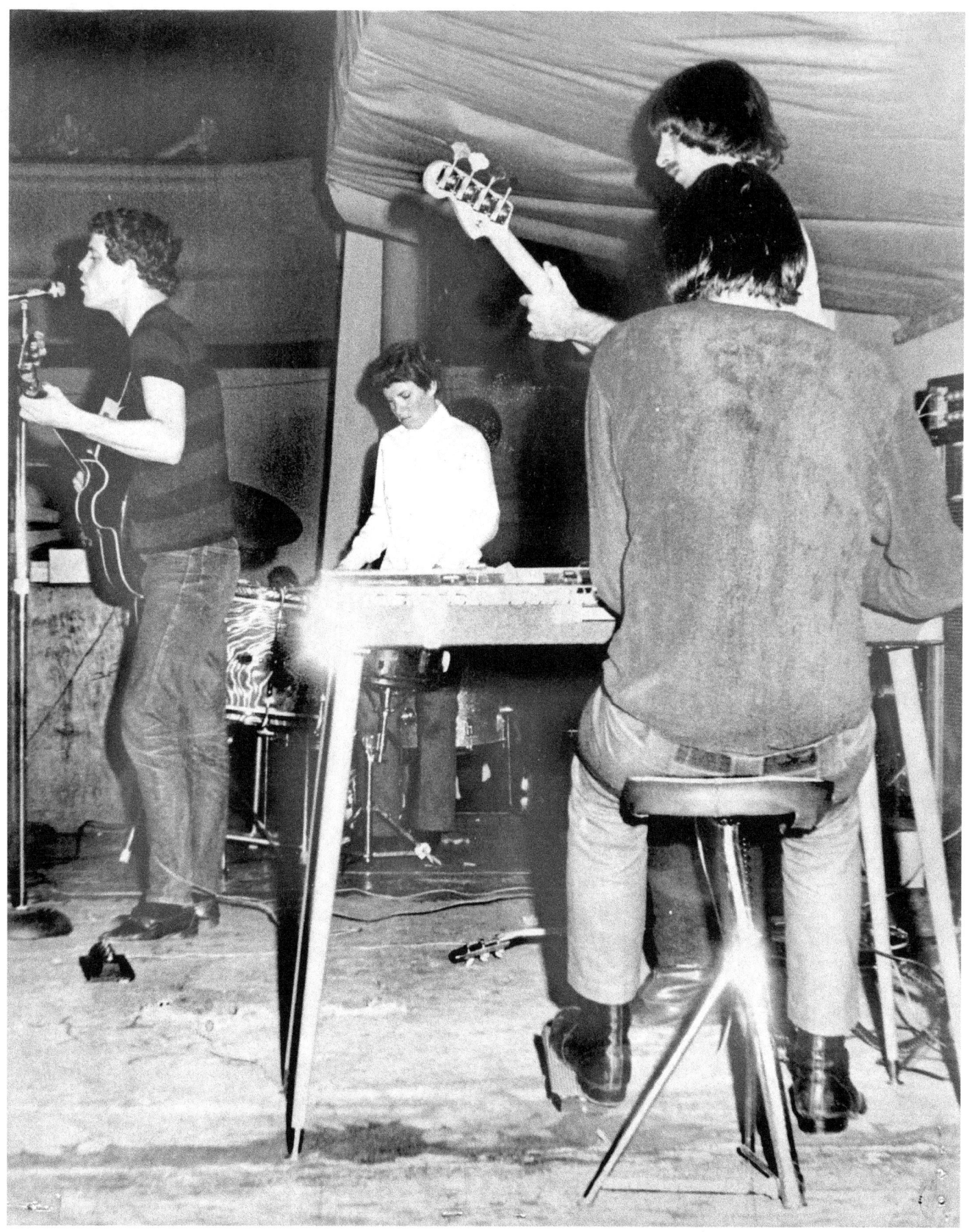
The Velvet Underground at The Retinal Circus, June 30, 1968.

www.ingramcontent.com/pod-product-compliance
Lightning Source LLC
LaVergne TN
LVHW081359060426
835510LV00016B/1894